THE
ROBERT MCRUER
MEDICINE READER

THE
ROBERT MORLEY
BEDSIDE READER

THE
ROBERT MORLEY
BEDSIDE READER

Robert Morley

HENRY REGNERY COMPANY·CHICAGO

Library of Congress Cataloging in Publication Data

Morley, Robert.
  The Robert Morley bedside reader

  1. Morley, Robert—Biography. I. Title.
PN2598.M67A3 1975 790.2'092'4 [B] 75-29027
ISBN 0-8092-8130-9

First published in Great Britain in 1974 by Robson Books, Ltd., London
First published in the United States in 1976 by
Henry Regnery Company
180 North Michigan Avenue, Chicago, Illinois 60601
Manufactured in the United States of America
Library of Congress Catalog Card Number: 75-29027
International Standard Book Number: 0-8092-8130-9

Contents

A
MUSING
MORLEY

Preface ,

Robert Morley is what the English have instead of Leonardo da Vinci. Which is a matter for considerable regret, if you happen to be Italian.

Mr Morley is a kind of frivolous Renaissance Man, a creative obverse to those industrious blokes who would spend the morning on their backs atop some scaffold sloshing chiaroscuro on a chapel ceiling, the afternoon chiselling thighs from marble, and the evening nailing sonnet sequences together; and it depends entirely upon your view of polymathy whether you feel it more worthwhile to have painted ambiguous giacondas for the souvenir trade and invented the helicopter than to have made civilisation roll in its various aisles for nigh on half a century by every comic means available.

For Mr Morley's every limb and digit is occupied in the service of comedy. Not only does he bestride English humour, he also has a finger in every pie of it: he dramatises it, he acts in it, he directs it, he produces it, he presents it on stage, on film, on television and radio, he declaims it aloud after other people's lunches and dinners, and he writes it down in the myriad magazines on both sides of the Atlantic fortunate enough to have wooed him to their pages. More than this: he embodies humour, he exudes it through the billions of pores that dot that gigantic surface of his. No one who has sat waiting in the stalls for the marvellous upstaging entrance that Mr Morley invariably writes for himself will ever forget the magic exhalation upon which this huge preposterous galleon is borne in. He always starts a furlong up on the field, he is launched on the laughter that the audience has been waiting to pour out, there is this tremendous comic goodwill that goes out to him from the rows of crimson plush.

Privately, for those of us privileged to have him more or less to ourselves sometimes, he is exactly the same. The man comes into the room, and the room changes. I have eaten many meals in his matchless company, and can testify that Robert Morley has done more for mediocre cuisine than all the grands vignobles put together; informed by wit, he passes the information on with effortless generosity. Nor does the generosity confine itself to the mere distribution, it is a quality with which Mr Morley is imbued and which therefore, since the style is totally the man, gleams everywhere in his conversation and his prose: his malice is defused by fun, his satire is warm, his deft dismemberment of others is always executed with the same scalpel he takes to the monstrous ego which it is as much his delight to deflate as to puff up in the first place.

His writing, of which this is the first anthology to be published, has all this and immeasurably more: a great nostalgic, Robert Morley will annihilate bogus sentimentality with one adroit word; he will defend romance with reason, and make truth ring out on laughter; he will indulge himself utterly and yet share that indulgence so delightfully that it becomes selfless; he will make arrogance a scaffolding from which to construct some baroque comic point, then kick that scaffolding down to reveal it for the temporary convenience it was, because he is a master of caricature and the self-portrait is his chef d'oeuvre.

He has a giant's impatience with irritating trivia, which is why he is sometimes taken to be petulant when what he is really doing is defining his personal limits of significance: the contemporary world through which Robert Morley rolls, watching, is awash with minutiae, and he knows very well the dangers this insidious rubbish can create if we do not keep it in its place. We must live on a larger scale, is what he consistently implores, we must see the grand sweep, and live in it with gusto and fun and energy and a pervading awareness of the daftness of so much that threatens us. Life must be larger than itself, if it is to be worth living.

If it is as large, in every possible sense, as Robert Morley, then there is no question but that it will be.

ALAN COREN

xii

Foreword

There is nothing I enjoy more than writing for the papers. I am one of those all-purpose, occasional hacks, ridden by editors for short distances along well-worn trails. 'Morley,' they ask, 'write me a thousand words on the best dinner you ever ate, or could you do a piece for us on falling down on the ice?' I make a point of obliging. Where I know a piece of mine is to be published, I make haste to secure a copy, although I remember perfectly what I have written. I read it avidly, fearful that the editor might have deleted a sentence, the compositor misspelt a word. When I was a child, I would carry home my school paintings with the same pride with which I now display my work to anyone who has the time or the inclination to read it.

Here, then, are some of the pieces which I have written over the years, a diary without dates. I have always wanted to keep a diary, but though I have bought many, could never discipline myself to fill their pages. It was not that I lacked the time so much as that I never found the right time. On the way to bed I was too sleepy, waking in too much of a hurry. Besides, I only write when I know someone is waiting to read.

When I was a child it was far easier to resist education than it is nowadays. There were no 'A' Levels opening the door to perpetual boredom in an institutionalized world. I left school at sixteen with an unfilled mind, sublimely unconscious of what others had written in the English language and with a profound ignorance of the classics, of mathematics, geography, history and foreign tongues. I had a hatred of solving problems to which others already knew the answer. In what proved to be my last term at school I was given some substance to analyse by the Chemistry master and was flogged for refusing even to light the Bunsen burner. 'You know what it is,' I told him, 'I don't, and what's more I don't bloody well care.'

A difficult child doesn't necessarily grow into a difficult man. I like to think I am more tolerant now and I certainly have little excuse left for churlishness. I have lived the life I wanted to live in the country where I chose to be, with those I have loved and who have loved me. What more can a man ask? Only, perhaps, to be read. It may seem strange therefore, to dedicate this book to an English master at Wellington College whose name I have long since forgotten, but who I think loathed the whole place almost as much as I did, but who to set us thinking or just possibly to get a little peace and quiet for himself, set essays and awarded cash prizes. In those days half a crown was a fortune. It bought five strawberry messes at the tuckshop.

1974   ROBERT MORLEY

FOLKESTONE
AND
FATHER

Trailing Clouds of Treacle . . .

Anyone who has ever been stowed away in an ambulance will, while the operation is actually being carried out, have glimpsed on the faces of the spectators a look of shocked enjoyment. It is the same look as I experienced in my pram during the first few months of life. People peered at me as though I had been the victim of an accident, and so I had — the accident of birth.

I had a difficult birth, and after an anxious eight hours for all concerned, mistook the doctor for my father. I remember lying perfectly still with my eyes closed in a chill of terror. 'My God!,' I told myself, 'I've landed right in the middle of it.' My mother lay in a euphoric trance at having produced so splendid an infant, and I could not, even if I had wanted to, disturb her complacency and exhaustion. I could only lie there and shudder.

The doctor was not my idea of a father. I remember I particularly disliked his hands. I was not introduced to my real parent for some hours. It was not the fashion in those days for fathers to attend the birth of their children, and I approve of the modern attitude in this matter. The least a father can do is to welcome his offspring in person. I am all for coming out into the drive to greet my guests. I do not expect them to find their own way into my study.

In point of fact I was a singularly beautiful baby — all ten-and-a-half pounds of me. They don't come that size any more, and it was with justifiable pride that my mother handed me over to the nursery staff. Nineteen hundred and eight was a good year for my father, and we could afford a nursemaid as well as a nanny. I remember them both perfectly, although neither stayed with us for very long, my father's affairs calling, as they did so frequently, for sudden retrenchment. In those days we were always moving house. My sister claims it gave her a sense of insecurity; even now she is loth to move around; travel, except local, is out of the question. Me, quite the reverse. I am

1

always planning to go to China. One of us must have got it wrong. Our moving around was perhaps fortunate, as the farm where I was born was burnt to the ground soon after we left it. It had, after all, perfectly fulfilled its function. My father at the time dabbled in and dreamt of champion saddlebacks. How amply I was to compensate him for his early failures in that field, although he was not to discover until some years later that he had produced the greatest ham of all.

My father was the sort of father who upset treacle on the table-cloth to amuse his brood. Quite early in my life he had the disconcerting habit of lifting me high in the air. Babies do not on the whole like being lifted, and none of them care to be dropped. I don't say my father ever dropped me, but he came damned close to it. He lived until I was over thirty, a life of extraordinary crisis and financial adventure, full of alarums and excursions. He never understood money, but believed, like his son, that this was because he could never get his hands on enough of the stuff. He was in turn soldier, café proprietor, night-club impresario, club secretary, farmer and postal poet. He was often a bankrupt, always a gambler, and of all the excitement, happiness and occasional despair he brought me, I remember him best sitting pretending to be asleep, a handkerchief over his face, and four, sometimes even five chocolates arranged on his lap, while I, choking with pleasure and the effort of restraining my giggles, tiptoed towards him to seize a sweet while he feigned unconsciousness. Then he would wake, remove the handkerchief, look down with astonishment, count the remaining chocolates, and express bewilderment, rage or resignation before once more replacing the handkerchief and pretending to nod off. If there has ever been a better game, I certainly have never played it, and if I was honest I should say that the only acting I ever learnt was at my parent's knee.

But back to the nursery, the boredom of starting tea with bread and butter, and the constant delight of Keplers, a patent medicine much favoured by my parents, which along with Parrish's Food, kept me and my sister fighting fit, or at any rate fighting. We fought with each other, with nanny, and later with a selection of governesses. We were apt to boast, the two of us, that we could get rid of any governess within a fortnight of her setting foot in our nursery. Later, my parents despairing, or possibly unable to afford the redundancy settlements, sent us to a dame-school at the end of the road. It was a long road, and halfway along it a dog barked menacingly at my approach. It was my ever-present terror that one day he would detach himself from the chain to which he was shackled, and tear

2

into my ample and defenceless rump. I did everything I could to avoid alerting him. I walked in the ditch, I tiptoed along the road, I stooped beneath the hedge, I played truant. My mother poo-pooed, my sister jeered, my teacher scolded, and I grew up terrified of man's four-footed alleged friend.

Looking back on my first few years, I realise now they were ones of continuing anxiety. At six I craved chestnuts to bore through and thread on string. I hurled a stick one afternoon at a chestnut tree and brought down a couple attached to a small branch. Instantly at my elbow a lout appeared, threatening to tell the owner of the tree. He bluffed me out of sixpence and made me promise to meet him the next Saturday for a further contribution. I have forgotten now whether I did or not, but I remember the terror of my first experience with guilt and blackmail. As usual I overstate the case. What I experienced, I suppose, was being found out.

Nobody found out much about me when I was a child. There wasn't perhaps a great deal to learn. I survived to tell the tale, to hold my own grandchildren on my lap and to try to remember how my father looked when I play the chocolate game. I resist lifting them high in the air. I never tickle them. (God, how I hated being tickled!) On the rare occasions when I preside at tea-time, I give them cake first. There is no logical reason not to do so. When my grand-daughter is older I shall try and persuade her never to curtsy when shaking hands. I dislike 'manners'. I avoid finding things for them to do. I lived in an age when children were always being given simple tasks. I have never forgiven Mrs. Boddam Whettam who, when I was a child, once gave me seventeen invitations to a bridge tea, to be delivered personally by one who was frightened of dogs, who was shy of strangers, and who loathed exercise. Fortunately we were living in Folkestone at the time, and I climbed to a rocky pinnacle of The Leas and let the wind carry each invitation separately over the cliff and out to sea, and when Mrs. Boddam Whettam waited disconsolately at her bridge parlour, the cards set out on the green baize tables, a marker and a pencil arranged in every place, bravely blinking back her tears, I never gave her a thought. I was sitting in the Electric Cinema watching Charlie Chaplin playing the same scene far better on celluloid.

Bath Chairs, Governesses and Patent Medicines

In Folkestone I still expect to be patted, to be recognised as the little boy who delighted them all in my sailor suit. I like to return whenever I feel the shadows beginning to lengthen, to ring the doorbells of the houses and explain to whoever opens the door that this was where I lived when I was a child. We were always moving round in Folkestone. We left The Leas and set ourselves up in Augusta Road. We had a house in Earls Avenue and another in Turketel Road, not at the same time, of course. We weren't rich by Folkestone standards. If there's one thing young people lack today, I am afraid it is Folkestone standards. It may well be what's wrong with the country. Who today rides in a Bath chair? 'I think,' the doctor would say, soon after the spots disappeared, the rash faded, the temperature subsided, 'I think he could go out for a little, in a Bath chair.' And in a Bath chair I went. The very best Folkestone Bath chairs had folding mahogany shutters with windows through which one looked out onto the patient back of the attendant, silently plodding ahead. With the shutters drawn one was insulated from the noise, a silent world with the delicious uncertainty that one might have suddenly become stone deaf. It was necessary sometimes to open the shutters and shout, just to reassure oneself. Mother steered from the back. Convalescence was achieved slowly, thoroughly, but achieved. Young people nowadays never get a chance to get better in Bath chairs. What's lacking is 'style'.

On Sundays the bands played on The Leas. The bandstands were situated at some distance from one another, but it was possible, by positioning one's Bath chair accurately, to listen to the Grenadiers with the right ear, while the Marines enchanted the left. No wonder I am not fond of discotheques. I was spoilt in my youth by the real thing.

What gave Folkestone, and in a sense myself, character, were the

4

cliff-hangers, the lifts. I travelled in them on an average at least once a week, always my heart was in my mouth. It is this sense of danger that makes life sweet. I am numbed by the blaséness of astronauts, those laconic voices revealing their boredom. Even their names appear to me subnormal — Pete, Greg. My sister, who is called Margaret, and I, who was christened Adolf, used to scream loudly just before take off. Count-down was signalled by closing the sliding doors, and then there would be the terrifying surge of water. We would look up at the seagulls circling far, far overhead, at the tiny figures in the car which was about to crash down on our heads, and scream. Of course, it never really hit us. We used to pass the car halfway. Sometimes it would be quite full, whereas our lift would contain only my sister, myself and our governess. I always wondered whether they adjusted the weight of the water, how it was that we rose and they sank without unseemly haste, while the balance was so unequal. At the top, splash-down was always carried out without a hitch. The car was accurately positioned to enable us to step out of it and hurry home to tea.

Our governess was called Miss Faithful. She was called a lot of other things as well, by which I mean she didn't keep changing her name, it was we who changed our governess. My sister and I simply couldn't keep a governess. They came and went. We used to stick pins in them. What idiots they must have been to desert their posts, to cry halt. What trouble they caused my parents by deserting so frequently. But despite the incessant upheavals, the comings and goings, dismissals, resignations and engagements, my father and mother never lost hope, never surrendered to the modern and quite ridiculous assumption that parents can raise their own offspring.

What singles my generation out is this lack of coarseness so prevalent today. Young people are no longer refined. They never had a governess to show them how it should be done. For if our governesses had anything in common besides a deadly loathing for my sister and myself, it was this air of ineffable refinement, evinced in every action which they allowed us to observe, and which they encouraged us to emulate. The washing of hands, for instance, before every meal. They never held their fingers under the tap, or left a smudge on the towel. Soup spoons travelled outwards across the plate, bread was crumbled, toast was cut, butter was spread evenly. Tidiness was maintained, handkerchiefs were kept in sachets, pins arranged symmetrically in pincushions, bookmarkers placed between pages. Our governesses were always prepared for inspection, and they tried to keep us similarly at the ready. I wonder sometimes what was

5

the reason behind the rule. Why did they insist on everything always being in its proper place? Was it only because when it was time for them to pack and go, they would know where everything was? And why did they go so often? There are pictures still in existence of my sister and me at various ages — dear, jolly little things we seemed — but not to our governesses.

When I undress at night I let all my clothes slide onto the floor — the big shelf, Miss Kipps used to call it — and there they stay until morning. My clothes seem to last as long as everyone else's. They may have to go to the cleaners more often, but I have saved hours of my life through defying Miss Kipps and not arranging them neatly on a chair, or hanging them in a cupboard. But what of the generation who never knew Miss Kipps? What pleasure would it be for them in middle age to let their clothes lie around? Or if it comes to that, to hold their hands under a tap, or not even to wash them at all? They will be simply doing what they have always done. They will never know the pleasure of not doing what they were brought up to do.

For in the tight little world in which I was hatched and reared, there was tremendous security, a security largely unknown today, and based I think on three great faiths — Keplers, Dr. Parrish and Syrup of Figs. These were the three great patent medicines which no household could afford to be without. Keplers was imbibed after breakfast. There was a special Keplers spoon kept in the medicine cupboard. A delicious treacly substance which wound itself out of the jar and down the gullet. Parrish's Chemical Food was taken through a glass tube, otherwise, legend had it, one's teeth turned black. The excitement of this ceremony could hardly be exaggerated. As the tube was clenched between the teeth, one entered the world of Jules Verne, H. G. Wells and R. L. Stevenson. The mixture thus assimilated, one handed the tube back and hurried to the glass to examine one's teeth. Syrup of Figs never quite managed the rapture of the others. It was always offered in a spoon overlarge for the mouth, had a tendency to spill and stain the pyjamas, and because one had already cleaned one's teeth, was seldom followed by a sweet. One had to content oneself with a throat pastille. Bath chairs, governesses, patent medicines made me what I am today. How sad that the younger generations would infinitely prefer to be without any of us.

A Kensington Childhood

Long ago when smokeless fuel seemed as improbable as moon exploration, my town was known as The Smoke. Visitors came to London to experience the fogs. 'Is this,' they would ask each other, 'the genuine pea-souper?' Then, coughing enthusiastically, they would grope their way to Baker Street and the lodgings of Sherlock Holmes. But fog such as Dickens knew has gone the way of Derry and Toms, and if you ask who Derry and Toms were, I have forgotten. They were people who once kept a shop, people like Mr. Gunter who made brown bread ices, and the lady who sat outside Kensington Gardens, a hundred balloons above her head, the strings clutched in her hand, defying the winds to bear her away before she had disposed of her work load. Why didn't she take off and, floating just above our heads, crash into the Albert Memorial? I suppose because Albert would not have been amused.

No child brought up as I was in Folkestone and Kensington Gardens ever felt the need of a psychiatrist. Today adventure playgrounds have taken over, and children are expected to hang upside down like bats or tunnel like worms or swing like monkeys. We were expected to behave, to keep off the grass. There were occasional lapses on my part of course, like the morning I walked fully dressed, or rather fully uniformed, for I was wearing my first sailor suit, into the Serpentine, by permission of my father. Perhaps he hadn't really believed I would take him at his word; perhaps he was just tired of me whining that I wanted to paddle; perhaps he wasn't even listening. At any rate, with full parental approval I strode forward until the water encompassed my thighs and then, realising that all was not as it should be and that my trousers were clinging and impeding my further progress, I attempted to retrace my steps, lost my nerve and finally my footing, and started to scream. 'Come quickly,' the crowd told each other, 'they are drowning a child in the Serpentine!', and gathered at the water's edge to boo my parent and console me. It was the first great drama of my life, but there were more to come. A few years later I was carried into the house we lived in in South Kensington on a stretcher. I have never forgotten the way onlookers regarded my recumbent form. There was still a vogue, at least in our drawing-room, for the picture that told the story, the physician comforting the parents of the dying child, the lonely colonial opening the mail with the postman on horseback retreating over the hill, the ruined spendthrift, head down on the kitchen table, a revolver within reach. Anyway, I wished there was an artist who could have captured that moment and titled it 'The Invalid, or Back from School'. For school it was that caused my health to crumple. I was always allowed home in mid-term with acute melancholia from horrific boarding-schools named after some saint, and where the sufferings of early Christian martyrs were cunningly reproduced — flagellation at St. Wilfrid's, starvation at St. Christopher's, conflict with dragon at St. George's. Do I exaggerate? I think not, but in London at least I never went to school. London was sanctuary. I ran home, I was carried home, I was sent home, and I was safe at least till next term.

Every now and then, when I have a spare hour to kill, I find myself again in South Kensington. I walk once more around Courtfield Gardens and pause outside Number Seven, the earliest sanctuary of my childhood. Here my grandmother lived on seven floors, not that she ever climbed the stairs to the attics, but must often, I suppose, have descended the stone flags leading to the basement where the work was done. My grandmother ran a tight ship, with a first mate called Hinchley. When Grandmother lay in her huge bed, dressed for dying, she took formal leave of us all. One by one we were summoned by Hinchley, one by one kissed and admonished, and given our last sweetmeat from her hand, and then she would reach up and tug the great wide bell-rope behind her head, and Hinchley would usher us out. There was no reason to ask for whom the bell tolled, Grandmother tolled it for herself. When she did die, the whole of Courtfield Gardens was strewn deep with straw to muffle the sound of the horses' hooves and the carriage wheels. If, when I die, I crave anything, it is not a memorial service but the village street covered in straw.

We inherited Hinchley, but not for long. Ours was a different household altogether and my father, a Piccadilly gambler, couldn't keep a silver canteen, let alone a household. In our rough days we lived for a time at the Naval and Military Hotel in Carrington

Gardens, nearby. My mother hated above all one Christmas we spent there while she hunted among the small change in Father's pocket for enough to give the staff their Boxing Day tips. We were very poor that Christmas. We moved around a good deal, never further west than Gloucester Road, never, alas, further east than South Kensington Station. In Gloucester Road, Bailey's Hotel, a huge and rather splendid building with a glass portico and porters at the ready, reassured and comforted us when fortune was at its lowest ebb. Had not this great enterprise been named after my uncle, Sir James Bailey, who had in some mysterious way commanded it to be built? He was dead before I arrived on the scene, and his huge fortune gone astray, distributed piecemeal to what my father called the collateral side of the family. But then of course Sir James was only an uncle by marriage, having espoused my aunt Elizabeth rather late in his life, but comparatively early in hers. The match, so they said, was made at the behest of the curate of St. Jude's whom and where my aunt worshipped.

We would sometimes take tea at Bailey's, in which we still took a proprietorial interest, dreaming of the day perhaps when Father's ship would at last come home, along with the winner of the two-thirty, and we would simply repossess. We never, naturally, had the same *folie de grandeur* about Harrods, where my grandmother had shopped when it was still just a small fishmonger's shop and Mr. Harrod in the traditional straw hat would leave the sluice-board and come to the carriage to take the order. People stayed in their carriages in those days, even when they visited, or left cards, as the ceremony was called. Sometimes they didn't even bother to accompany the coachman on his rounds with the engraved slips of pasteboard. He just dismounted from the box, hastened up the steps, slipped the cards through the letter-box and was away before the horse got restive. If my grandmother was in the carriage, a footman came as well, but even so my grandmother never alighted, just gave her card to the fellow, with one corner turned down to indicate she had been prepared to descend, had the circumstances warranted it. The hostess would sit in her drawing-room in splendid isolation and the cards would be brought up for her inspection, and then scattered on the silver salver always standing in the hall. It saved on the teacakes and the washing-up, not that that was of course the object of the exercise. But what, then, was the object? I simply cannot tell you.

I only know that as I walk around, I miss Lady Gorringe's brougham in which we would travel on Saturdays to Whiteleys to 'buy chocolates. Her Ladyship never stopped in other departments, or imagined we would want to linger among the toys or even the tropical fish, although we had to walk through both departments before coming across the confectionery counter. Once arrived, we would buy three one-pound boxes of comfits and return to the security of the carriage. Bayswater, in Lady Gorringe's book, was no place to loiter. It just happened to have the best sweetmeats. When the boxes were empty there was a way of tearing the paper glued to the inside to simulate exactly the firing of a Maxim gun.

I miss, too, the smell of the Tube, as it was called, a hot, not very pleasant, but completely exciting smell; the threshold to pleasure, for we only took the Tube for an excursion away from the territory — to Brompton Road to shop, or to Down Street to watch a procession, both of which stations have vanished, although for a long time they remained ghost platforms at which no train stopped and no passenger alighted. In the war, Brompton Road Station was the headquarters of the London Air Defence Operations. From there orders were issued each night to haul down the barrage balloons and send up the night fighters, and a girl who is now my agent pushed model Spitfires across the maps and became General Pyle's Personal Plotter. For Down Street there was no such honourable retirement, or if there was I was never told.

But long before all this, when I was still governess-bound, I believed Piccadilly Circus meant what it said, and that in the centre of my town, in the centre of the world, was a perpetual display of acrobats and tigers, bareback riders and performing seals, and when I at last discovered quite late in life that this was not the case, the shock was traumatic. I was on a bus, an open bus with wooden seats and individual mackintosh covers which fixed with studs and straps to the sides of the seats. We circled the Circus and I asked if for once we could get down and inspect the menagerie, even if we couldn't see an actual performance.

'But this *is* the Circus,' they told me, 'don't you see, it goes round, a circus goes round!'

'But what about Oxford Circus?' I enquired, with panic gripping my heart.

'The same,' they told me, 'only you don't go round Oxford Circus, you cut across it.'

I knew then better than to ask about the others — Holborn, Cambridge. In a moment I had lost not one but four great pleasure domes.

I preferred the top of the bus whatever the weather, not because I was ever an open-air child, but because from there I could look down and read the names on the marquees outside the theatres and cinemas we passed. I would announce the attractions in as uncommitted a voice as I could muster, not because I wasn't dying to alight and watch Ronald Colman in *The Garden of Allah,* but because I knew any request to do so was doomed to refusal, and I hoped passionately that my parent, guardian or whoever was accompanying me on whatever errand would abandon the plan of the day, or at any rate postpone it long enough for us both to alight and spend a few magic hours of excitement. Indeed I may claim, I think, to have been one of the pioneers of subliminal advertising.

I don't know what determined my father that it was time for me to know something of the world, nor can I remember at what age he guided my steps towards Chinatown, which he had reason to believe was situated in Limehouse. Had he waited a bit longer he would no doubt have settled for Gerrard Street, but it would have robbed us both of a long and exciting journey through the Docks and eventually reaching the Causeway which my parent was, I think, as surprised to discover as I was. He had only the shadowiest idea of how to pass the time until we could return the way we had come, and we wandered around aimlessly staring at the few Chinese who passed.

'I suppose as we're here,' my pater remarked suddenly, 'we might see if we can buy some snow', and then, since it was in the middle of summer, and sensing my surprise, he explained that by snow he had meant to indicate cocaine. 'This is where they sell it,' he told me, and taking my hand in a protective gesture which always embarrassed me, he entered the local friendly neighbourhood store. To his delight the old woman behind the counter was unmistakably oriental of countenance.

'Good afternoon, Mother,' he began, much to my astonishment, 'Mother, I wonder if you could tell me where I might find some snow?'

The old lady regarded him with the composure native to her race. 'Snow?' she asked, 'Did you say snow?'

'That's right,' my father leaned forward, hot on the trail.

'We had some last winter,' she told him.

'Ah, last winter. But not now? I wouldn't want much,' Father assured her.

'You won't get much this time of the year,' she told him patiently.

There was a long silence after that, while they stood staring at each other and then it was I who took Father out of the shop and led him away. 'I don't think,' I told him, 'she knew what you were talking about.'

'Nonsense,' said Father, 'she knew all right, but for some reason, she didn't want to sell. I expect she thought I was a plain-clothes Bobby.'

One adventure was enough for Father, besides it was time for cards. We took the bus home.

It mustn't be thought that my parent concentrated his efforts on educating me solely in vice. On the contrary, he was anxious that I should grow up an officer and gentleman and as unlike my aunt Sophie as possible. Aunt Sophie had once flung his *Ruff's Guide to the Turf* into the fire in an effort to stop him dissipating any further her sister's fortune. He never forgave nor forgot. My aunt was religious. 'How would she have liked it,' he would observe, when recalling the incident, 'if I had burnt *her* Bible?' To nurture my taste in horseflesh, Father would take me on Sundays to Tattersals Repository on Knightsbridge Green, which was in those days the Sotheby's of the Sporting World. Every Monday a sale took place in the vast Palladian Courtyard and the day before, Father would view the savage brutes. He was forever opening horse-boxes, entering and inducing the tethered creature to move over. I never knew what we were going to find — gigantic shire-horses, excitable hunters, clumsy mares in foal. All I knew and dreaded was the fact that sooner or later I would be menaced by their heels and have to take to mine. Father knew no fear. After all, had he not been a cavalry officer, if only for the briefest period? On Sundays he returned to the world of his military prowess. Clutching his catalogue and occasionally waving it to induce a horse to show its paces outside the box, led by a groom whom my father rewarded with a florin, he would estimate the price which 'Lot Seventy-Three, the property of a nobleman and regularly hunted with the Quorn and sold only because she is not up to the owner's weight' would fetch next day under the hammer.

He never, as far as I know, actually attended the sale, perhaps because he feared he might be tempted to buy a horse and hitch it to a lamp post outside the Naval and Military, to add to my mother's anxieties.

I learnt a lot from my father, but not perhaps the facts of life. Once and only once did he ever attempt to educate me in such matters. We were walking along Jermyn Street and my father suddenly choked on catching sight of a youth walking daintily on the opposite pavement.

'Bobbie,' he told me, when he had recovered composure, 'I am going to tell you something very dreadful, something you ought to know. There are men in this street who paint their faces.' I looked

12

round eagerly in search of Red Indians and saw none. Oddly enough, I never walk down Jermyn Street without thinking of my father.

But each night before the curtain rises, while I am painting my face, I never think of him at all.

The Club Secretary

Our hall porter is back from shooting grouse on the Chairman's moor and my club is open again for business. I have always been extravagantly proud of club membership. To find oneself at least in theory acceptable to judges and dukes bucks me up. Besides the obvious advantage of somewhere free to wash and brush up and even get a little of the ready when I am up from the shires, the main attraction for me is that club life gives me a chance to mend my manners, to be gracious and become more like the Queen Mother. The Queen Mother syndrome is what keeps us clubmen going. On crossing the threshold, the hall porter welcomes each member with such deferential loyalty that he has him looking round for a lady-in-waiting to whom to pass on the bouquet. There isn't a bouquet, naturally, in my case, just a few bills and a polite reminder from the Secretary that a coffee-room account remains unpaid. But then, to have a coffee-room account at all is a sort of bouquet.

It is good for us every now and then to switch off 'Hadleigh' and 'Upstairs, Downstairs' and try that sort of thing for real while we still can, to practise speaking to the staff and lifting gin and tonics from silver salvers. But surely, you might argue, you can get the same sort of workout at the Savoy? To start with, if you yobs had ever been to the Savoy you would know that the waiters take the drinks off the tray themselves and announce the price. In clubs there is an appreciable pause before money is discussed, and in olden time, tucked beside the elegant goblet on the silver salver, the change from a sovereign in laundered silver. Nowadays of course there is no change, so the Maundy ceremony has been discontinued.

Nevertheless, there is still a world of difference between catering staff and club servants. I should know — my father was a club secretary, my father-in-law actually owned his own. After the First World War there was a perceptible swing towards having waitresses in the

14

coffee-rooms. It was, some sociologists affirm, one of the very early manifestations of the Women's Lib movement. These early pioneers, although not exactly liberated during working hours, allowed a certain measure of fraternisation after working hours, and my father, who was employed in those days in one of the more traditional establishments, was always suggesting to the committee members that an evening à deux with the wine waitress did not help things the next day, when the claret was found to be corked. But his protestations went largely unheeded and it became increasingly difficult to keep up the high standards of pulchritude and service demanded by the members, so frequently did the staff avail themselves of the opportunities thus afforded to go A.W.O.L. and better themselves in private service. The matter was finally resolved as far as my father was concerned by his threatening to dismiss the next goddess caught in flagrante delicto, and being dismissed himself by the Chairman after an unexpected confrontation in the Carlton Grill.

The Carlton Grill, dear me, what a long time ago this all happened, and even before then I was no stranger to club life, for my proud parent used to smuggle me into the Cavalry Club while he was temporarily running that establishment, to watch the peace processions after the First World War. The Cavalry was best for getting to and from processions because of Down Street Station round the back. I never pass The Cavalry without hearing again the military bands and the crunch of horses' hooves on the gravel. If I should ever forget which doorway shelters its members, there is always outside it the taxi and the lean, bowler-hatted fare lifting off one of the few remaining genuine leather suitcases in all London, and preparing to carry it, along with the ritual furled umbrella, up the steps.

My father's favourite club was the Orleans, which had a rather daredevil reputation for gambling and the best food in London. My father was always nervous of my manners when we met in the Orleans. I used to wait in the hall for him, along with a King Charles spaniel who was more or less permanently chained to a radiator, and had his own drinking bowl. I never did discover for whom the dog was waiting, but I used to talk to it occasionally, and whenever I did, the porter would raise his eyes from the A.B.C. in which he was habitually engrossed, to give me a disapproving glance, intimating that non-members should not talk to members' dogs.

My father-in-law's club, when nepotism allowed me to join it years later, was a good deal more a home from home. A home from a rather superior home, of course. My father-in-law seldom ventured out of the beautiful old house in Clifford Street which housed not

15

only princes, prime ministers, masters of foxhounds, selected film-stars and merchant bankers, but Mrs. Hillsden. Mrs. Hillsden was no ordinary person, she was accustomed to tempting royal palates, having been trained in the kitchens of the great Mrs. Keppel herself. My mouth still waters at the memory of her chicken pancakes. Her fishcakes left nothing to be desired, the only fishcakes I ever ate which justified the claim. Fishcakes, in my book, are the ultimate test of culinary prowess and Mrs. Hillsden passed with flying colours. She also, of course, had a flying temper, and my father-in-law, afraid of no member, sometimes claimed he ran the club entirely to keep her in good humour. 'If all the members were to resign tomorrow,' he would observe, 'it wouldn't matter a great deal. If Mrs. Hillsden went, it would close the club.' Sometimes, but not too often, he would allow his grandchildren to romp around the Ladies' Annexe at lunch, and when the time came to say goodbye, insist that their hair should be combed and their faces sponged before they proceeded downstairs to pay their duty to Mrs. Hillsden. 'We don't want Mrs. Hillsden to see you looking like that' became a statutory admonition in the family.

His attitude to his members was that of a headmaster going though a difficult period in the school's history. Certain boys had been made prefects. He was particularly fond of any pupils connected with transport and afforded them special privileges. He was always expecting to take a journey himself, although in point of fact he never did, and believed a man at the top would facilitate his progress when the time arrived. Privileges at the Club consisted of being able to get a private table for luncheon, and he would award these on a merit system known only to himself. Prime Ministers were not always favoured, or even trusted. One evening I once sat with him in the annexe after 'lights out'. 'Lights out' used to be fairly early, to enable Mrs. Hillsden to catch her bus. Locking up on this occasion was impeded by the continued presence of Mr. Macmillan and his guest in another part of the club. None of the staff quite liked to urge him back to 10 Downing Street. The hall porter consulted the proprietor, who considered the matter with an anxious frown. 'I suppose,' he observed, 'if he is trusted to run the country, he can be trusted to lock up. Give him the front door key and ask him to slip it back through the letterbox.' Then, as the porter was leaving, he was recalled. 'Perhaps not,' my father-in-law told him, 'Bring me the key. I'll do it myself.'

A club is a great leveller of the ego, once you're elected, of course.

RECOLLECTIONS
OF
A
RESPONSIBLE
GENTLEMAN

Counting the House

Audiences, like salad dressings, are never the same twice running, or five hundred times running, if it comes to that. I am often accused of playing the same role too often. My defence is that I play each audience only once. Younger colleagues, and most of my colleagues are younger, hold that an audience is not there to be played with, that an actor's duty (however evocative the phrase) is to play with himself. The challenge for them lies within. Scofield, Gielgud and Olivier are high priests ministering to the faithful, while my role is that of a potboy serving my customers with gin and tonic. My patrons are a fun-loving bunch seeking a night out. They seldom leave the premises with the hushed reverence and sober mien of those who have had an Experience. They walk into Shaftesbury Avenue wondering about supper, or a bird, possibly both.

For me the supreme excitement each evening is the moment of truth. The Manager is in a dinner jacket, I in my underpants, the audience in the bars. The curtain has fallen on the first act. There is a sense of excitement, of ritual. I am invited to bid for the house. I have already decided on a figure. During the first scene I have not been idle. There are certain vantage points on the stage, certain moments in my performance when I am able to glimpse specific parts of the auditorium and note the empty seats gleaming in the dark, reflecting the lights from the stage. It is this play of light with which I have to contend. From certain positions I am inhibited from sober calculation. From others it is comparatively easy. But of course I am never stationary for very long. The closest analogy, I suppose, is with a pilot on a bombing raid. By the interval, my mission is completed. I am ready for de-briefing. I hazard an estimate, tear open the envelope, and read the figure written on a small square of notepaper. Sometimes I am spot on, on other evenings miles off target. I haven't allowed for parties at reduced prices, or hospital nurses in disguise who haven't paid at all. Purists may argue that an actor cannot give of his best whilst engaged in mental arithmetic. I can only say that I have found it a help not only to be able to do two things at once when I am actually on the stage, but to have two things to do. It was Marie Tempest who told me that she had never played a scene without at the same time being able to make out the laundry list. 'Naturally,' she added, 'I don't make out the laundry list myself these days, but I still could.'

The excitement over for one evening, I am ready for the second act. Now that I know the quantity of the house I can start to worry about its quality, which indeed may have changed drastically during the intermission. Often an audience which begins by appreciating every nuance and laughing at exactly the right moment and for exactly the right length of time, will finish the evening in sullen lethargy and hostile silence. On the other hand, a house which begins by not laughing at all, and driving the actors to despair by coughing itself silly in the early scenes, may end up as our particular pride and joy, laughing uproariously and applauding wildly. Our fault or theirs? I can never be sure. All I know is that every audience has to be watched every minute of the evening. Take your eyes off the customer, turn your back and the brute springs. I once asked a circus proprietor her opinion of lion tamers. 'Any fool can do it,' she told me. 'Only a fool does.'

One thing I learnt early in my job, miracles seldom happen. When I owned a racehorse I would watch it go down to the start, telling myself that despite the opinion of the trainer, the jockey and the travelling lad, there was nothing to stop it winning. But there was, and it didn't. It's the same when a play isn't going to win either, but as long as the race is on, there's hope. Every night when you get to the theatre you tell yourself that it might be full, but it never is, though oddly enough it is never quite empty either. There is a fixed number of determined masochists who attend performances of a failure each evening, spacing themselves with mathematical precision. There is no reason why they shouldn't all come to see you on the same evening − even then they wouldn't fill the theatre − but their singular task is to prolong the agony for yourself and the backer and nobly they achieve it. What Providence ordains that there should be just so many chartered accountants, foreign diplomats, provincial librarians, licensed victuallers, engaged couples, consenting adults and lapsed clergymen assembled each evening in the fauteuils? For us it is *you* who are the real performers, the jugglers, the acrobats, the roustabouts.

As we survey the motley crew of pickpockets who jostle each other afresh every evening in our tent, we are grateful for your infinite variety, without which it would be quite impossible for us to remain your faithful, humble and obedient servants.

Elegy Written in Kensal Green Cemetery

I stood on the extreme edge of the grave, gazing down into the camera. Pillars of the British stage shared my vigil, a genuine vicar intoned the service, at just the right moment the earth was sprinkled on to the lens, shutting out our faces. 'Cut!' called the director, and we were back in our camp chairs in a trice, resuming the crossword puzzles and the aimless chatter of actors on location.

'I thought so-and-so was dead.'

'Oh no, Denville Hall.'

'Did he actually marry the girl?'

'I don't think he was prepared to go as far as that.'

'Did anyone catch Keith Michell last night?'

Over our shoulder we could glimpse Vincent Price, hideously deformed and made up as a grave digger, shovelling in the earth and reciting Shakespeare.

Kensal Green Cemetery, if it has lost a little of its prestige as a top person's burial pad, is riding high with film directors. They say Ken Russell never shoots a film without a sortie round the mausoleums, and what wonderful mausoleums they are. Even in Victorian times, some of them must have cost a bomb. Many of them are large enough to entertain in, although ours seemed to be the only party going on that day. The pigeons flew in and out, the wire defences erected against them having long since rotted. Bats nested and waited, in vain as it happened, for Vincent; this is not a remake of Dracula, but a film called *Theatre of Blood*, a ghoulish tale of an actor's revenge on dramatic critics and, in my case at least, their pets. I play all my scenes with a pair of whitish poodles nestling on my lap. Anyway, that's the theory.

What makes Kensal Green so alluring as a setting for death is the general air of sustained desolation. So different, one murmurs to Vincent, from your own dear Forest Lawns, where everything is tidy

22

and ordered. Here the blackberry bushes are six foot high, the nettles giant size, the headless angels crumble before one's eyes. It is not so much a case of 'This too shall pass away', as 'This too has passed away'.

How carefully the Victorians ordered their demises, how exact the lettering of the inscriptions, nearly all the esquires star-billed, their wives in slightly more modest face, the children, at any rate those who had died young, consoled with a motto — 'God Called Early' or 'Lent Briefly'. The achievements of the men were noted with modest satisfaction, their earthly addresses afforded enormous prominence. 'Of Greystones, Guildford in the County of Surrey.' Men may die, but Guildford must remain in Surrey, surely. It would be amusing, I opined, to engrave a stone for a prodigy. 'Andrew Wilkins, Esq. Grand Chess Master, at one time Warden of the Worshipful Company of Skinners, Late Viceroy of India. Born Dec. 1892. Died March 1895.'

Nobody seemed very amused. The dogs came back and I carried them a short distance and then put them down on the gravel and hoped they would follow the leash. Naturally they didn't. We moved the lady who looked after them behind the camera, and they bounded joyfully towards it.

We worked on and on, because one of the actors wanted time off to go to the Garden Party. There were a good many jokes on the Cinderella theme, and finally a hired pumpkin arrived and he drove away to excited waves, and the rest of us had luncheon. It was the sort of meal top people eat once a year at the Albert Hall, while being lectured by Ustinov or Clement Freud on how to stay in the hot seat and keep your cool.

I am not one for the box lunch. The chicken seemed even more tired than I was, and apples are not my idea of a pudding, although no doubt they appeal to the purist.

We had just discovered that there was no beer, and sent Vincent as the star away to negotiate (he is really the most amiable of monsters) when the hearse arrived. Not our hearse, that was already in place for the next set-up, but a genuine hearse, containing presumably a genuine corpse, and accompanied by genuine mourners. The latter got out of their cars and surveyed the scene with amazement; took in the actors gnawing on chicken bones and dressed, some of us at least, as they were, although of course there were others hideously made up, with bandaged legs and matted wigs, who were playing Vincent Price's familiars.

There was also all the paraphernalia which accompanies a film unit, the brutes and the bashers and the reflectors, the camera trucks and recording vans and the crew, the casual bystanders and in this case even the director's children dressed in stars and stripes, and everywhere on the bushes, on the tombstones, in the nettles, on the grass banks, on chairs, on tables, even held in the hand, a vast harvest of paper cups in full bloom.

The mourners stared at us and we stared back. There was nothing either of us could say. Had we, I wonder, spoilt their grief, intruded on their privacy, frightened them out of their wits, or just conceivably reminded them that in the midst of life is death, or is it vice versa? I shall never know.

After a time they got back into their cars and drove away, with never even a glance at us, and we went back to our idiot task, and horses appeared and dragged bodies along the gravel, and we looked suitably shocked, although we knew the body was really a dummy, and the actor it represented even now perhaps shaking hands with the Monarch. We counselled him before he left on no account to admit he was making a film, because it simply wasn't true.

The shadows lengthened and the assistants went round urging everyone to get on with it while it was still light, and gradually tempers began to fray and suddenly a marvellous row burst upon us. They stood there, trading insult for insult, two middle-aged buskers rather too well known for the fray. Sometimes one would hurl what we feared might be a final epithet and walk a few paces away and then suddenly, inspiration returning, walk back and deliver what he hoped might be the coup de grâce. There was no physical violence, because both feared for the make-up and hair pieces, but it was immensely exhilarating while it lasted. How rarely nowadays does one see a good fight or listen to men who have lost tempers, shouting their hearts out.

The rest of the day passed tamely, even my poodles seemed to flag, and no longer to care at whom they looked. Finally it was over and the producer thanked everyone, always a sign some of us should have been on overtime and weren't, and we climbed into our cars and left Kensal Green Cemetery behind. Lucky, I suppose, and thankful we were still able to do so.

But I shall go back, not to be buried I hope, but to struggle through the blackberry bushes and tread down the nettles and read the inscriptions on the tombs and wonder when they shovelled Great Uncle Frederick under the earth, whether they congratulated him and themselves on having chosen just the right spot and just the right building and just the right text, and whether they had left just enough room for Great Aunt Matilda. I'm sure they had. The Victorians may not have understood death better than we do, but by Heaven, they enjoyed it more.

The One That Got Away

*How The Other Half Loves chalked up two years and 800 perform-
ances at the Lyric Theatre, London, and during its run there grossed
over half a million pounds. It was translated into half a dozen
languages, and ran successfully in at least four of them. Why did this
particular play flourish in the theatrical jungle?*

In April, 1970 there seemed little point in going to Leicester, where
How The Other Half Loves was being given a second chance at the
local repertory theatre, the first production of the play at Scarborough some months before having satisfied neither author nor
management. The invitation had come from Peter Bridge, whom I
knew only slightly, and for whose managerial prowess I had little
enthusiasm. On the other hand, I had to find myself a play and a new
management. The firm of H. M. Tennent, with whom I had been
closely connected for much of my theatrical life, and I had come to
the parting of the ways.

The split, for which I was entirely responsible, came during the
run of *Half Way Up The Tree*, a play by Peter Ustinov, the success of
which in the West End had not been repeated in other countries
where it had been produced. I am never slow to apportion credit to
myself, and regarded the whole episode as a personal triumph for my
acumen and theatrical know-how. I had saved Ustinov from himself,
and with the very considerable help of the director John Gielgud,
had once more pulled Beaumont's* chestnuts out of the fire.

He must, I was sure, be grateful to his old friend, so that when I
needed a quick thousand pounds, I approached full of confidence
and goodwill. I had taken it upon myself to raise a few thousand
pounds to buy and equip a school for autistic children and contacted

* H. M. Tennent's managing director.

26

a number of the rich whom I considered would be fairly easy touches. There are men in our business who give, and men who don't. Lew Grade, for instance, is a natural giver. I approached him across a crowded room and sniffed his cigar for a time while he told a story. I am not a good listener to other people's anecdotes, and after a time, thinking, or perhaps just hoping, that he had reached the point, I asked him for the money. 'Of course,' he replied, 'you shall have it in the morning. Don't interrupt,' and went on with his tale. On the books of ATV Lew owes me very little. Indeed, I must have cost the company a small fortune in my unsuccessful attempts to launch a series on their network. But Lew Grade is a generous man, not given to jobbing back. I am not praising him. I don't think generous men should be praised, they are the lucky ones.

Another of my successes on this occasion was John Lennon, who whipped out his cheque book and gave me the bread on the spot. I hardly knew John Lennon. On the other hand I thought I knew Beaumont, and when he refused me I was shattered and very angry. I felt he owed me something. He felt exactly the opposite. When I told him that if he didn't give me the money I would sit in his outer office till he did, he seemed only mildly amused. When, this ploy having failed, two days later I told him that unless he gave the money I would never darken his door again, he called it blackmail, which it was. I am not a reasonable man. I have never forgiven him. I trust I never shall. When I told my wife about the incident, she looked nonplussed. 'My darling,' she told me, 'whatever made you think he'd give you the money? He's not a friend of yours', and of course he isn't. Friends are not made out of mutual obligation.

What finally decided me to go to Leicester was a race meeting at Stratford-on-Avon, where a horse of mine was entered to run. On the map Leicester seemed fairly close. There was a time when I knew every provincial city in England. I spent ten years of my life on tour, but I had forgotten Leicester. In any case it appeared to have been re-planned recently with multi-storey car parks to depress me with their cement understains and crush barriers to keep back non-existent crowds. The object of the exercise is that you should drive straight through such cities these days without stopping, or indeed noticing that they are there at all.

I was surprised to find the theatre in a bus depot, but I suppose even that makes sense in a way. A handy sort of house with raked seats and a flat stage, the convenience of a curtain was dispensed with, so that when the furniture had to be changed halfway through the first act, an entirely separate production was mounted with a ringmaster and uniformed circus hands. The audience enjoyed it hugely. I thought they quite liked the play. After the performance several patrons accosted Robin Midgley who had directed the piece, with advice on how to improve it. He struck me then, as he does now, as an eminently patient, reasonable and above all resourceful fellow. About the play I was not so certain. The most serious snag seemed to me that most of the goods were displayed in the first act, the climax of which was an immensely complicated coup de théâtre in which two players contrived to attend separate and simultaneous dinner parties.

'Is it, do you suppose,' I asked John Jonas who drives me around on these occasions and nurses me through the performances I do decide to give, 'is it, do you suppose, too clever by half?'

Mr. Jonas on this occasion seemed not to share my anxiety. 'A thoroughly good evening,' he insisted on the way home. 'I don't know why you didn't enjoy it more.'

I think it was his enthusiasm as much as anything else that decided me to go ahead. It was after all an even money chance, and this has always seemed generous odds to me. I had certain reservations, and having told Peter Bridge that I was game at least up to a point, tried for the next couple of weeks to get the play altered, but found Alan Ayckbourn, the author, fairly obdurate and inclined to prefer his own ideas to mine. I started out by demanding that the baby in the play should be replaced by an elkhound, and that I should be encouraged to participate in the celebrated dinner scene dressed in Japanese costume. Both suggestions were resisted tooth and nail, and on reflection correctly. After two years I can't pretend to have made much of Alan Ayckbourn, an eminently cautious fellow, not given to hanging round the cast, remembering the anniversaries of the play or bunching his leading ladies. About his play's quite phenomenal success he evinces little emotion, hugging himself, if he does so at all, in secret.

Having got me to agree to do the play, Peter Bridge's immediate tasks were to find the money and the theatre with which and in which to present *How The Other Half Loves*. The money presented no problem. There was an embarrassment of would-be investors. All he had to do was to circularise the list of prospective backers with which all managers provide themselves, and the eighteen thousand pounds for which he asked to mount the production was subscribed overnight. The Angels on this occasion smelt success. Both the author and myself had been previous winners over the course and almost uniquely Peter was able to produce two notices written by national critics on the strength of the Leicester production, predicting a London success for the play when it was eventually produced there. You could hardly ask for more, and no one did. Indeed one of the backers, Eddie Kulukundis, of whom we shall hear more later, tried unsuccessfully to provide all the capital required from his own pocket.

Without the Sunday notices written by Bryden and Marcus it is possible that nothing much more would ever have been heard of the play after Leicester. The local notices for the piece were not particularly encouraging, and interest in a London production had all but ceased.

The problem of obtaining a suitable West End theatre was as usual more complicated. In order to appreciate the singular good fortune which attended its arrival at the Lyric, we must inform ourselves not so much about the state of the theatre in London and the provinces, as the state of the theatres themselves.

In a business which is by nature optimistic and essentially fly-by-night, the ground landlords of theatre land have been ever since I can remember in a class by themselves for sober mien and general lack of high spirits. Grave and reverend seigneurs to a man, they are the farmers of this never-never land of ours, always complaining of the harvest, but raking in the shekels whenever and wherever possible. In the years between the wars such men were typified by the late Stuart Cruikshank, who controlled the giant Howard & Wyndham circuit in the then flourishing provincial theatre. Here was a card-index man after the heart of I.B.M. itself. No employee however insignificant, no star however famous, no gown however dilapidated, no piece of scenery or property however unlikely ever to be used again, escaped his filing system. He once let me scan some of the cards on his desk awaiting re-deployment. 'Miss A,' I read, 'asks thirty, is worth half. Good personality and clothes sense, but poor personal wardrobe. Not a hard worker at matinees. Blonde (natural).' Then followed the dates she had fulfilled and the fees paid. The card beneath referred to a ball dress which although now alas damaged at the hem, was considered by E. J., who had supplied the information, as still suitable for second lead singer in the finale or ballroom scenes.

If there is one thing that theatre owners have in common it is a pathological horror of throwing anything away, for this would entail the purchase of a replacement. In the forty years I have been sitting around in dressing-rooms I don't believe I have ever sat in a new armchair. I have never used a lavatory which hadn't been designed half a century before, or looked into a mirror which wasn't lit by a

29

naked bulb. I have never seen a carpet in a corridor or a picture on a wall. The higher you climb in most theatres the more sparse the furniture becomes. Understudies are not encouraged to relax. They must sit for the three hours each evening on upright chairs, no two of which ever match each other. To strip an average theatre of its furniture and fittings, most self-respecting junk men would demand a fee. Since *How The Other Half Loves* opened at the Lyric Theatre, the landlords have recovered close on a hundred thousand pounds in rent, yet the window sash in my dressing-room which has been broken since we opened, and I am not at all sure wasn't broken when I played there in *The Little Hut* ten years earlier, is still broken. Does it matter? Well, the answer is it doesn't really matter all that much to the actors. It may be good for us not to be able to relax too much backstage, and we are used to such conditions, but broken window sashes and sagging armchairs are a symptom of bad management. They do little to dispel the belief that theatre owners in this country are a bunch of frustrated property developers who spend a good deal of their time flattening their noses against the grimy window panes and gazing out enviously across the street at the car parks and supermarkets which luckier colleagues have been allowed to build.

A theatre site is rarely a profitable one, particularly if one takes into account how much more could be made by turning out the actors and installing the business men and tourists. Yet these same tourists now come to this country in large numbers partly because of the theatres and it is the height of folly that the latter should be in the hands of vast conglomerates like Associated Television, who treat them like unwanted children, allowing them each year to grow a little shabbier and more uncared for, evincing no pride in their achievement, grudging them even a coat of paint.

However, when it comes to renting them out for profit, parental interest revives somewhat. Heads we win, tails you lose is the rule, and the empty shell, for such each house virtually becomes with every fresh lease, is let to the producing manager on the harshest possible terms. The average rent demanded is in the region of a thousand pounds a week against twenty per cent of the box office takings, whichever is the larger, and the lease can be terminated by the landlords two weeks after the takings drop below an agreed sum which is known as the 'stop figure'. Over and above that the tenant is expected to pay for light, heating and staff and nowadays the landlords are chary of providing even a bulb, let alone a spotlight, so all this has to be hired afresh. The landlords, however, insist on retaining the right to sell programmes and operate the bars, an enormously

30

profitable business. One might be forgiven for supposing that they are often more concerned with the brand of whisky on sale in the foyers than the brand of entertainment advertised on the marquee.

Not all London or provincial theatres find themselves in this sorry state. There are producing managers who maintain their establishments in reasonable repair and one house especially, acquired some years ago by Peter Saunders, has been extensively redecorated and redesigned. The Vaudeville Theatre shines forth like a good deed in this naughty world. But these theatres are not as a rule available to managers such as Bridge. Their proprietors prefer to have a finger in the pie if they have not actually baked it themselves, and do not as a rule let their theatres on a strict rental basis. Bridge was now free to proceed at his peril, the date when he would be able to conclude negotiations for a theatre some weeks off, and with no guarantee that he would get one at all, should business in the West End suddenly spurt. He could find himself as he did with his recent production of *On The Rocks*, up in the clouds circling the airport without permission to land, and if the tour proved financially disastrous, running out of gas.

Rehearsals began on my birthday at the Irish Club. I had not then, and still haven't, the faintest idea what normally goes on at the Irish Club, apart from the sale of *The Irish Times* in the hall, but I climbed the stairs to the room reserved for the first rehearsal and found Bridge had invited a few press photographers along for a drink in the hope that they would take pictures of myself cutting my birthday cake. There is surely no duller subject for portraiture, or one an editor is more easily able to reject, than an actor poised over confectionery, but the attempt has to be made.

Robin Fox turned up and I was as always reassured in his company, and managed the ritual bonhomie and drank the champagne, blissfully unaware of the impending catastrophe. A few days later I was to learn that my trusted friend and manager had terminal cancer and the shadow of his approaching death made life suddenly much colder. In the evenings after rehearsing I would drive down to the King Edward Hospital at Midhurst for a picnic in his bedroom, bearing caviare and curious mousses from Fortnum's, and drinking champagne by his bedside. It didn't really make matters better, but in times of crisis I find extravagance sometimes helps me. Late one evening I left him and walked along the corridor to where a nurse sat at a table, writing reports on her patients.

'I'm off now,' I told her unnecessarily. 'I gather the news is rather good about Mr. Fox. They haven't found anything sinister.'

She didn't answer for a moment. I had caught her, I suppose, off guard. Into her eyes came a look of disbelief, instantly checked by a professional caution.

'Oh yes,' she said, 'Mr. Fox is doing very well', and that as far as I was concerned was that. I never again had any hope at all.

It was at the first rehearsal that I met Eddie Kulukundis and learnt he was to be a partner in the enterprise which Bridge, possibly scenting battle, had christened Agincourt Productions Ltd. My first impression was that of a large, untidy and likeable Greek who was constantly ducking his head in a basin, not to cool it, but to get his hair to lie down.

His recent impact on theatreland was already proving sensational. Word had got round that there was a stranger in town and back at the old saloon they were busy polishing the glasses and getting out the old deck of cards. Here was a tenderfoot aiming to join in the poker game and there was no lack of players anxious for him to draw up a chair and sweeten the pot.

They found out almost immediately that he was a man after their own heart who never seemed quite certain of how many chips he was betting. When I asked him once how much a particular hand had cost him, he assured me he would break even.

'Come now, Eddie, what do you mean by even?' I persisted. 'You think you'll lose five thousand?'

'A bit more than that,' he told me with a smile. He is a good loser but then, of course, he's had a lot of practice these last two years.

He is the only son of a wealthy Greek shipowner.

'I suppose you would call us wealthy,' he told me. 'As a boy I lived in Wembley; it's not all that rich a neighbourhood. On the other hand my father always had chauffeurs.'

'Chauffeurs?' I queried.

'One at a time. Mother's dowry when she married — we Greeks have dowries, you know — was twenty thousand, a lot of money in those days.'

Mother was strict with him, I gathered. Until he was twenty-two he didn't go out with girls. Then, as is often the way, it all happened too quickly. He fell deeply in love and for the first time really started to go places in his father's business. He managed the English branch from the Minories. He made a small fortune, intent on marriage and settling down possibly in Wembley himself, although by this time the rest of the family had moved abroad. Eddie, as the son of the eldest brother, was more or less the boss.

'There's not,' he explained, 'much difference really between a

32

good shipowner and a bad shipowner. In good times everyone makes money because they can't help doing so. In bad times we all lose.' He was not, however, to find the same conditions prevailing in the theatre.

Eventually his girl chucked, and Eddie surveyed his life and didn't much care for the way it looked. For one thing the cousins were growing up and began giving him advice on how to run the business, and for another he had been working so hard he hadn't really had much fun. He is not a man who relaxes easily, or one that makes friends without effort.

'I am the one,' he told me ruefully, 'who is always the host. It was the same in ship building, I pick up the check. Perhaps I go out with the wrong people — out-of-work actors, struggling playwrights. I don't seem to like the company of the sufficient, the rich, the people in society, English society. I like American society.'

'Do you,' I asked, 'know many people in American society?'

'Not really, but I think I get on better in America.'

In point of fact, last time Eddie was there he got on rather badly. He went with Bridge to produce *How The Other Half Loves* in New York.

'I intended to have only a small investment,' he explained, 'but Bridge suggested I subscribed the whole British capital, and insisted when we arrived on Broadway there would be plenty of backers eager to take most of my share and pay me a small premium for the privilege. Things didn't turn out that way and the other backers didn't show.'

In the event the production was a disaster and the money was lost. With the English profits, Eddie reckons to break about even over the entire venture, but is understandably resentful.

'I kept telling myself that in the event we didn't get the money subscribed, I had had too small a stake in the London production, and as after all this was my first real success maybe I should play up my winnings.'

If unrequited love was the main reason why Eddie decided to live it up in the theatre, he would perhaps have done better to stick to girls. After two years he has very little to show for the two hundred thousand pounds it has cost him to date.

He claims he knows more about the business. 'This time last year,' he confessed, 'I was strictly a sucker. I couldn't say no.' It started with *The Happy Apple*, a play which had a moderately good reception at an outlying theatre and Eddie went to see with one of his girl friends who thought a visit to a theatre might cheer him up. He met the director, heard of a vague plan to transfer the piece to the West

End and stepped straight on to the ice. He didn't present it himself, but put up eighty per cent of the capital required. He got his first sight of a theatre balance sheet, was fairly startled and has remained in a mild state of shock ever since. He finds it surprising, for instance, that managers with whom he presents plays should transfer so high a percentage of their office expenses to his production account. When he rents a playhouse he doesn't, or at least didn't, expect to have to pay several hundreds a week over and above the agreed sum for the illuminated signs directing patrons to the theatre. When told he can mount a production of a play already in the repertory of one of the National Theatres for four thousand, he is dazed to find his production bill has shot up to twenty thousand because the scenery has deteriorated through damp and the dresses have been claimed back and rented out afresh by the costumiers to amateur groups. The mistakes on Eddie's bill do not amount to a great deal when one considers the account as a whole, but they serve to irritate him. He is gradually being weaned from the theatre. 'If I could find a nice girl and marry her, I'd give it up tomorrow,' he told me, and I rather hope he does.

Meanwhile he flits from function to function, automatically accosted, perpetually propositioned by those who seek his patronage and his fortune. 'In point of fact,' he told me, 'it's not strictly true that I still have to pick up the checks. Quite often I get a free lunch and there's really nothing to pay at the cocktail parties. All I have to remember to do is not to take my cheque book.'

When I asked Bridge why we were rehearsing at the Irish Club, he told me proudly that coming up from Berkshire every morning I would find it easier to park. 'On the first night,' I told him, 'I am expected to make a speech excusing our state of unpreparedness on the grounds that we are all keen motorists?' I hate rehearsing in rooms as opposed to on stage. I find the space confining, the stage management sits on top of you, prompt book in hand, my mind wanders, reflecting on the decor, marvelling that people normally carouse in these surroundings, give wedding receptions and children's parties. Public rooms are haunted for me by the ghosts of failed functions.

I seldom enjoy myself at rehearsals. I am back in the classroom I so hated; the director is a beak, sometimes a decent beak, but a beak nevertheless. This is his hour, his month in fact. We normally rehearse for about that long. He is here to see we do the work as he wishes it done. Some actors suck up to the master, follow him around, take his hand on the walk, call him Sir, bring him flowers. I

34

am not one of them. Between him and me there is always hostility of a kind often manufactured by myself. I am stimulated by conflict, like to be the one who hurls the rubber while he is intent on the blackboard. In all my theatrical career, only Guthrie willingly enslaved me. I longed to please him, accepted his rule absolutely in triumph and disaster, and no one brought the temple down more effectively on occasions than this curious Irish giant whom I met almost at the outset of my career, who directed my first two plays and later myself in *Pygmalion*. I had stepped into the breach at the last moment, learnt Higgins in a weekend, gone on ill-prepared and triumphed at Buxton of all places, or so I thought. He came to the dressing-room afterwards. 'Very dull,' he said, 'most of it.' It seemed like praise, perhaps it was intended to be. He never bored one, was never bored himself, stopped in time, dismissed the class, sent us home for prep, a lovely man. When he died, his bailiff came to his wife. 'The great tree has fallen,' he told her. On the morning of his memorial service at St. Paul's, Covent Garden, the tree in the church-yard fell. There was no wind. A great director.

Of course I have liked some of the others, some of them I suppose have liked me, but not many. Peter Brook I found hell. I never understood what the fuss was all about. He tried everything to get me to do what he wanted, I did everything not to. We even quarrelled about who should fetch the Coca Cola. Perhaps because of him, perhaps despite him, *The Little Hut* was a great success, but I don't think either of us would ever go through it again. To enjoy oneself is the supreme duty of an actor. I cannot bear the rack of effort, if acting doesn't come easily I'd rather it didn't come at all. I cannot bear dedication when it is paraded in front of me. I like my director corked, but frothy. The late Jack Minster was the flattest director I ever knew, and the most amusing. He sat in the stalls, wrapped in an overcoat and sustained despair.

'Don't look on the floor,' he would tell us, 'there's nothing there but the play.'

'It gets a laugh,' an actor would expostulate.

'I didn't hear it,' he would reply, 'I was deafened by the ones who weren't laughing.'

Peter Ashmore directed me in *Edward, My Son,* and *Hippo Dancing* and *A Likely Tale.* I enjoyed it. Willie Hyde White summed him up. 'What a civil little chap. I find him invaluable, always ready to fetch the script when I've left it in the Rolls.' But Ashmore was cleverer than that, cleverer with me than anyone else has been. He came into money and wisely didn't press his luck after that.

Directors are alchemists, their hour is brief.

Gielgud I admired enormously, but the trouble was everyone else did the same. I was perpetually comforting the cast in the wings during rehearsals of *Halfway Up The Tree.*

'I don't think John likes what I'm doing,' they would sob.

'Has he said so?'

'No, I just sense it.'

'I like it,' I would tell them, but the tears didn't stop. After a time I began to resent it. He did rather take Ustinov's side at the beginning, but luckily Ustinov wasn't there most of the time. I like a director to take my side. I demand it.

Midgley took my side from the first. I've got so old now that I am no longer a challenge to directors, just something they wish they could move around and can't. Which is not to say I don't make concessions. I made one or two. I didn't interfere with the casting, except to insist that Tetzel played my wife. No one seemed all that keen, not even Tetzel. She had done *The Little Hut* with me, so was more or less prepared. It's strange about Tetzel. I worked with her before the war in radio in New York City when she was only a child. She was the darling of the networks because able to play opposite any leading man in the Rudy Vallee Hour. French, British, Japanese, she took them all on and I never forgot her astringent poise. When I decided to play *The Little Hut* I told Beaumont about her, adding that I hadn't seen her for twenty years and she was possibly out of the business.

'She was in my office this morning,' he told me, 'suddenly turned up out of the blue.'

'Grab her,' I insisted, and he did.

It was the same with *How The Other Half Loves.* I hadn't met her or heard of her since *The Little Hut* finished more than ten years before. On the day I agreed to sign the contract, I lunched with Robin at Wilton's. 'The girl we need,' I told him, 'is Tetzel. Where has she gone, do you suppose?' That evening I walked into a cocktail party, the first one I'd been to for seven years, and there she was by the door.

'Do you want to do a play?' I asked.

'I might.'

As is usually the case with playwrights who deliver their plays into my hands, Ayckbourn began to grow restless quite early on. He had already seen his play rehearsed twice before and had fairly set notions of what it was all about. At the back of his mind, as indeed is nearly always at the back of authors' minds, was the idea that he had written a more significant play than I gave him credit for. Moreover

36

he insisted that all the characters except perhaps my own were fundamentally unlikeable. This didn't do for Tetzel. She was not as far as she was concerned playing a bitch and had no intention of doing so. The final confrontation was to come later at Leeds, but meanwhile there was a certain amount of muttering on both sides. I have always held that to make a steady income in our business, which should be all actors' ambition, one cannot afford to play unsympathetic parts. However much praise is lavished on you by the critics, the audience gradually comes to associate you with the unlikeable characteristics you have assumed in the cause of art. After a time they simply won't pay to go and see you. With the notable exception of Vincent Price, who cheats outrageously, few heavies grow rich. Tetzel and I were quite determined on this point. 'If they don't like us,' we told Ayckbourn, 'they won't come, and where will your little play be then?'

The other leading lady, Heather Sears, seemed much more disposed to go along with the author than we were. Heather, and subsequently Mary Miller who took over from her after a few months, both believed they were in a piece which had something to say quite apart from the laughs. They both spent considerable time with the director establishing the character. They were ready to discuss, for instance, whether the girl they were portraying read the *Guardian* before the *New Statesman,* and how many goldfish should be in the goldfish bowl, and the sort of toys they would provide for that off-stage baby. By this I don't mean they inaugurated the discussions or wasted time unduly, but they chatted around with Midgley whenever the opportunity presented itself. Midgley is a great chatter, but he is also a workmanlike director who runs a very successful theatre in Leicester and knows the curtain has to go up some time. On the whole he held the balance fairly between those who wished to find truth in the play and those who wanted to know where to stand, or more important perhaps, where the others in the cast were intending to stand.

Donald Burton played Heather's husband, and I never quite understood where he stood. He always arrived at rehearsal carrying a furled umbrella which was also a swordstick, and with a scarf tied high round his neck, reminding me of the late Queen Alexandra masking the dewlaps. He is a very good actor who also, as far as I am concerned, breaks all the rules in that he insists on altering his appearance for each role he undertakes. In my view quite fatal. They must know who you are and what you are going to do as soon as you step on the stage, in my book. Donald Burton on the other hand seems to invite them to ask which part he played. His great passion in life seems to be lighting. I don't mean what most actors mean by lighting — how many of the spots one can appropriate — I mean domestic lighting. He claimed to be able to lie in his bath and adjust the dimmers so that the perfect Mediterranean effect was achieved on the soap suds. I was always taught not to fiddle with current in the bath, but he seemed to come to no harm. Similarly, from his bed erotic effects could be created, and even the dawn simulated when it was time for the guest to leave. I hoped he'd ask me round to his pad, but he never did. I don't think he liked me very much. Perhaps he recognised a fellow egomaniac, or realised I would never be able to discuss dimmers seriously. I like the lights full up all the time, but will allow imaginative directors to keep them low until I burst into view, after which the rule, if I am allowed to make it, is light, light and still more light.

The other two members of the cast were Brian Miller and Elizabeth Ashton. Both having been in the original production at Scarborough, Alan decided that the parts could never conceivably be better played than by them, and he was right. They knew exactly what they were up to from the very beginning, refused to be swayed or disturbed by the uncertain manoeuvering of the rest of us and held firm. I cannot imagine what would have happened to the play without them. The rest of us used them as anchor buoys.

After a week rehearsals moved to the Haymarket, where Midgley could sit in the stalls and leave us to get on with it. But for some reason he seemed to prefer a chair at the side of the stage. I have never known a director who sat so long on top of a company. Otherwise I had no fault to find with him, or with the script. Normally I am a glutton for re-writing, but after my initial failure with this piece I thought it best to bide my time, say the lines the author had written and only when I found they didn't work with an audience, get him to alter them or preferably alter them myself. Directing is like cooking in the sense that all the dishes should ideally come to perfection at the same moment. Some actors boil almost immediately, while others take ages to rise.

There comes a time, too, when all of us demand an audience. 'Mummy, watch me,' we cry, and if Mummy isn't planning to visit the nursery for another week, the squabbles are liable to start. At the end of the month we were just about ready. The curtains had been drawn, the stage set. Arrayed in our costumes, we awaited the arrival of the grown-ups. They could hardly have been more appreciative in Leeds had they in fact been our relatives. We didn't pack the theatre, but business built, and we were complimented in teashops. There is nothing the English dislike more than having to talk to people they haven't met. When it happens to an actor, he knows he is on a winner.

I used to drive to Leeds, put up at the Queens and come down after the performances on Saturday and be in my own bed at four. I do not choose to linger. As one gets older, time grows more precious. Years and years ago we travelled on Sundays in special reserved coaches. Long, slow journeys without restaurant cars, but always with a pack of cards and beer, sometimes sandwiches, sometimes we rushed the buffet on the stations where we halted. A pleasant sort of day, particularly if one was sure of digs on arrival. I knew most of the towns in England then, sad, dead slums like Rochdale and Oldham and gay, comfortable, happy places like Southport and York. Blackpool was best of all, but all seaside towns were fun, Bournemouth, Brighton, Morecambe, even Southend. I was twenty-one at Blackpool and had melon flown from Manchester for my birthday party. I was always a show-off.

I opened *Edward, My Son* in Leeds at a matinee on a Tuesday. It ran for four-and-a-half hours with the hitches, but I knew we had a success. In those days the Grand was truly grand, an opera house really, with goodness knows how many floors and a lift and an enormous stage. It was a number one date, full more often than not, and when it was full there was a lot of brass. The manager wore white tie and tails and was a V.C. You put your best foot forward when you stepped on that stage. You lived in the Roundhay Park district. There were plenty of good rooms with wonderful Yorkshire teas before the performance and hot suppers afterwards. There were bits of the city which were unexpected, Marshall and Snelgrove for instance, and Austin Reeds. If like me you had a bad memory, there was always the excitement of rediscovery. Round here, you would tell yourself, somewhere round here there is a shop window in which stuffed squirrels are skating.

But Leeds has changed and like Leicester it too has barricades in preparation for some future riot perhaps, or just possibly a pageant. There is a new complex near the theatre and a new hotel and I wondered if I should have done better to have stayed there. But hotel bedrooms grow ever smaller and I preferred to be near the station. The theatre had given Bridge a guarantee, and we stayed a fortnight. Business was not sensational, but above average. The Grand breaks a good many hearts these days. There was a note for me at the stage door, left by Leonard Rossiter, who had been there the week before. 'Help!' was all it said. One morning saw a glorious row on the stage. A last attempt by the director and the author to get Tetzel to play it tough. She held firm.

'Do you mean to tell me,' asked Robin, 'that you are not going to play the part as we wish it played?'

'Yes. If you want it played that way, you must get someone else.'

'Two someone elses,' I told them, relishing the confrontation. That was the end, more or less.

After a fortnight we moved to Nottingham, where once two theatres stood side by side, like elderly maiden aunts, but one has now passed on, her grave a car park, though goodness knows what is planned as a headstone. The other remains, a dilapidated recluse. 'Do not embarrass the management with requests for complimentary passes. If your friends will not pay to see you, you can hardly expect the general public to do so.' Is the writing still on the wall? I am not sure. Nottingham is still a Moss Empire controlled remotely from the Palladium in Oxford Circus. The dressing rooms are not numbered, but labelled with great names of the past, Barrymore, Irving, Tree, or is that Wimbledon, where we went next? I can't be sure.

It is in Nottingham that I hear Bridge has been offered the Lyric. By now the production has been evaluated by the head office, the reports are in. The head brass of course doesn't come itself, but somewhere in the chain of command is a warrant officer on whose judgement they rely. Years ago in the days when the libraries made deals and put down their money in advance, there was a faceless, anonymous taster to whom they appealed for a verdict. If he said buy, they bought and the success was a foregone conclusion. Once they had the seats, they pushed the show. In those days, too, everyone relied on Fred Carter. When you opened out of town he came along and if he liked what he saw, found you a theatre in London. On the try-out of *Edward, My Son* he waited till we got to Manchester.

'You can have,' he told me, 'any theatre you want in London. Which is it to be?'

'His Majesty's,' I told him, and so it was. My God, I felt proud. I didn't have the same pride with this one, but then of course I hadn't written it. I counselled Bridge to try not for the Lyric but the Apollo if he was offered a choice. He was and he didn't, and was right.

We still had three more weeks on the road, Wimbledon and Brighton, but these passed uneventfully. There was not a lot more rehearsing to be done, and no re-writes. Everything would now depend on the first night at the Lyric. The first night of a play in

London is still a formidable obstacle, the Beechers Brook of the National course. In recent years attempts have been made to modify the jump somewhat. The supreme confrontation is no longer sought by management, as used to be the case. Before the war, when the theatre catered largely for the stalls public, managers regarded their first night list as all important, and spent hours at work on the Sheet. The idea was to seat the critics in warm nests of appreciation, although taking care they should not be irritated by loud laughter and bursts of applause while they themselves were scribbling notes in the dusk. Some managers, like the late Gilbert Miller, prided themselves on knowing the social scene and which Marquis was talking to which Marchioness. Gilbert had a profound suspicion of princesses. 'If possible,' he confided in me once, 'I keep them out. They are too casual, like racehorses.' Beaumont is another who is a great expert on such occasions, leaving as little as possible to chance. He has been reported to carry a thermometer to check the exact temperature of the auditorium. But the days when first nights were great social occasions is over. In point of fact nowadays it is quite difficult to fill the house at all, and after the friends of the cast have been accommodated, the manager may be hard put to it to find a representative audience and not one composed almost exclusively of fellow managers, agents, film producers and television directors who have seen it all before and are not all that keen to see it again. This is one of the reasons why previews are encouraged. The actors get a chance of playing themselves in and the professionally interested need no longer all come on the same evening.

On the whole, *How The Other Half Loves* at the Lyric Theatre on the night of August 5th 1970 played much as it had been playing for the last six weeks and the notices, when they appeared, were with one exception uniformly encouraging. Only Harold Hobson in *The Sunday Times* was unwontedly abrasive. He reported that most of the cast gave performances which looked as if they had been recruited from the rejects of the annual pantomime in a backward village, or could he have written originally a backwoods village? We shall never know. By the time his notice appeared we were home and dried.

A Church Is Not A Theatre — Or Is It?

The show must go on or *Don't give them back their money whatever is happening* is the first principle of theatrical management. No Play, No Pay is another from the same book. My profession has long been credited with superhuman powers of endurance and it is true that most of us act better with a high fever or a raging toothache and feel better afterwards. 'Doctor Theatre,' we tell each other, smiling bravely, as we are driven away in the ambulance.

Managers know that the public can seldom distinguish between one actor and another and certainly not between one actor and his understudy. To the Chinese and the audience we all look alike. Two things keep an actor acting on these occasions, one is he isn't going to get paid without giving a performance; the other that his understudy may just conceivably give a better performance than he does. In the second case his fears are usually groundless. In point of fact most understudies haven't a hope in Hell. I know you've seen different in the Alice Faye movies, but that was long ago, and even the suckers know different today. An understudy is paid to hold the fort, not to break out and win the war. What the other members of the cast require is someone who will enable them to score in areas where up to now they have been repulsed. With the understudy playing, everyone else expects to chalk up a few extra laughs. When the cat's away the mice insist on their inalienable right to play. They are not going to welcome another pussy!

Of course when I was an understudy myself, I took a different and more liberal view. I had ambition and genuine belief I could do better than my principal. I once put matters to the test. At Nottingham in high summer and before a modest matinee audience I lavished a week's salary on bribing the actor I covered to absent himself. In his stead I gave an intensely memorable, utterly satisfying performance, and was sacked almost as soon as the curtain fell. They simply

42

didn't want genius in Nottingham in those days. I finished the engagement as the assistant stage manager, at a wildly reduced salary.

The show which, alas, every actor has to miss is his own memorial service. These are very popular nowadays, though not with me. I have left written instructions that under no circumstances is there to be one on my account. I don't wish to go to the grave haunted by the fear that no one would turn up.

True, the ones I go to are usually well attended, but I seldom enjoy myself. Perhaps I shouldn't expect to enjoy myself in church, I never have, and I put it all down to being forced to attend Divine Service twice a day all through my school days. I don't really feel at home in a pew. 'Forgive us our trespasses as we forgive them that trespass against us,' I used to pray in my childish treble, glimpsing through my fingers the master who was going to beat me on the morrow, and wondering what on earth he was praying about.

The same unease doesn't affect me nowadays in St. Martins in the Fields or St. George's, Hanover Square, or St. whatever it is in the middle of Soho where we actors customarily gather to pay our last respects to our departed colleagues, but I am not exactly easy here either. A church is not a theatre, but the seating is strikingly similar. At memorial services the front of the house is the responsibility of the Profession, the clergy take their place on the stage. True we are occasionally invited to read the lessons, or deliver the eulogy, but our performances tend to be muted. There is a noticeable lack of confidence at the lectern and in the pulpit.

Not surprisingly, if you are growing as deaf as I am, it is often difficult to hear.

Memorial services, too, always seem to be still in rehearsal. Only the clergy know exactly what is going to happen next; the rest of us shuffle from knees to feet and then find we should have been seated all the time. Before the curtain goes up, the late actor's friends play ushers. In the school play everyone has a part to act. Ushers speak in low murmurs, smile quietly, shuffle the mourners. No one can be trusted to walk up the aisle on their own, to find a place. While the organ plays, the ushers precede each of us in turn, carrying not a torch, but a sheaf of specially-printed programmes. There is also one on every seat and another beside each prayer book. The name of the deceased is printed boldly on page one. We can be sure the billing is as he would have wished at last, and for the first time we learn the other names he bore. A lady at the door asks our names, and we pretend not to mind. Years ago one of the newspapers used to publish the names of the ushers who were to take part, and the list would be carried by elderly and faithful theatre fans who, alas, are now all dead themselves, or at any rate past caring. 'Which are you?' they would ask, in suitably muted tones, and then put a little tick beside the name, to remind them that they had had their money's worth.

Just before the curtain rises, the ushers usher in the immediate relatives, and then relinquish their roles. The amateurs hand over to the professionals. Preceeded more often than not by a small choir consisting of half a dozen ladies in red mortar boards, the clergy take the stage. The climax of the play is, of course, the eulogy, spoken sometimes by the officiating priest, but more often by one of our lot. When this is the case, it invariably commences with the personal reminiscence. No one ever says 'I didn't know George, and I never wanted to do so.' What they say is 'I first met George when he had patently dined too well and was about to —' here a frisson runs through chancel and nave alike. Is indiscretion for once going to gain the upper hand? '— was about to help an old widow lady across the road.' Alas, the danger has passed. We all relax in disappointment. As the orator continues, we learn more and more about him, and less and less about poor George. This is not a fault of course confined to theatrical eulogies. Even Top People's obituaries when they appear in their house magazine, commence with some memory of the writer shooting tigers in Bengal, when from under the tethered goat leapt his friend the deceased.

'Neither of us,' it continues, 'were destined to be killed that day, but I think we both enjoyed our first encounter.' We don't in point of fact want to know what he enjoyed, but he can seldom resist telling us just the same.

When the eulogiser has finished, the actor climbs down from the pulpit, trying to look unassuming. There is a special sort of expression for such occasions. 'I don't want any nonsense. I have told you the truth about George as I see it. The fact that we are in church simply doesn't arise.'

When the priest is in charge, the eulogy seldom includes the personal anecdote. This is not because clergymen don't appreciate a good story, simply that this one has never met George, although he claims often to have seen him across the footlights. He is careful to stress the fact that although George never prayed, and never went to church even to read the lesson, he was in the fullest sense a Christian Gentleman, and his salvation is perfectly assured. On such occasions the church mercifully believes in a special relationship for actors where the Kingdom of Heaven is concerned. The relationship of which Nixon and Wilson once prattled so happily, adapted to showbiz, a procession of Equity card-carrying guitar players, streaming unchallenged through the Pearly Gates. Why not, pray? Who better than we can learn to play the harp?

If nowadays I find myself attending rather more memorial services than I would wish, here at any rate is an unlikely crumb of comfort.

THE
ROOT
OF
ALL
EVIL

Expenditure Over Income

Every so often I lunch with my accountant. Even as I write this sentence I am conscious of the smug complacency inherent in the statement. It is as if I had written 'every now and then I send a contribution to Oxfam or help a blind old lady across the road'. That's how it is. Sometimes we lunch at my club, sometimes at his. The atmosphere in both establishments is similar — polished tables, English nursery food, middle-aged waitresses, old port, Stilton cheese and a hesitant approach to the business in hand. My accountant seems to be more at home and to know more of his fellow members in his club than I do in mine. I am not sure which of us lunches more often at his club. I fancy he does, but such matters are difficult to determine. When I go racing I know that I can count on seeing certain faces in the Members' Enclosure. I wonder sometimes whether these same faces count on seeing mine.

Whether from a fatal lack of arithmetic knowledge or laziness, I have never managed to keep accounts. I seem incapable of jotting down the amounts I spend, either at the time or afterwards. I never fill in a cheque stub or keep a receipt. This now engrained habit of financial sloth and ineptitude has caused over the years a great deal of trouble to everyone except myself. Yet I was brought up fairly strictly as regards money matters. I was encouraged to plan how to spend pocket money and exhorted to save my pennies. I was given over the years an extraordinary variety of money boxes, but seldom managed to fill them. Very early in life I grasped the point that money can only be spent once. My mother was keen on repeating to me the Dickensian edict that expenditure over income creates misery. I believed her, and determined as a child of seven never knowingly to spend more than I had in the bank, with the result that I have ever since been scrupulously careful never to ascertain how much or how little money I have lying fallow at a given moment of time.

Some years ago, in a more than usually desperate attempt to settle matters with the Inland Revenue, I journeyed to Somerset House, accompanied by my long-suffering accountant, to be received by one of those senior officials who dwell in remote offices on the upper reaches, and whose contact with the public is both selective and peripheral. I had come to make something which I am seldom in the mood, or indeed position to make — a cash offer. It was naturally rejected as inadequate, but the interview, although brief, lingers in my mind, partly because of the sensational bulk of my personal file, and partly because of the extraordinary charm and unworldliness of my antagonist — a veritable Humbert Wolf of a civil servant. In the course of the negotiations I heard myself remark that 'as far as paying my way with the Revenue was concerned I simply couldn't manage'. I left Somerset House that day enriched instead of impoverished. I often think of that sad, dedicated man and the mildness of his retort to my absurdity. 'Some of us have to manage.' In his simple statement I found immense comfort. Here a pillar of the establishment, of the Revenue itself, acknowledged the existence of the goats. I do not expect to be praised for my financial untidiness, but I sometimes wish that my herd was not so continuously chided by the sheep and their shepherds. If everyone counted their pennies and saved them there wouldn't be anybody left to borrow, and where would the banks be then, I should like to know.

After lunch my accountant and I adjourned as usual to his office. When he first took pity on, and charge of me, he was more or less on his own. There were not, as there are now, too many partners in his firm to get on one envelope. In those days, too, he was situated in a single house. Now, like others who have multiplied and prospered, his letters have to be addressed to include all the numbers of all the houses in the street which his firm now occupies. Nevertheless, I hope if he reads this he will continue to believe that I am still grateful to him. We are all, I fancy, grateful to our accountants, at least until the day when the bailiffs arrive on our doorstep. My own has never attempted to disabuse me of the fact that he can do little but postpone their coming. The Revenue plays cat and mouse with actors, but I don't expect the kill to come just yet, particularly as we are still playing around the fiscal years of my middle age, which is what makes these post-prandial conferences so baffling and fascinating.

'Your income for the year '64/'65 on which Surtax is payable in January '67, has been provisionally agreed, but there are several points as usual outstanding; who, for instance, are Harrap Sinclair and Beadle?' The question is hopefully posed, and I struggle to return the ball.

'Harrap Sinclair and who?' I ask.

'Beadle, or it could be Bradley.' An assistant passes the bank statement across the table.

'It does look like Bradley,' I agree.

'You wrote the cheque yourself,' he reminds me. 'We have no record of the bill.'

'Where was I?'

The assistant consults a ledger. 'You were making a picture apparently on location in Weymouth.'

'So I was,' I tell them. 'Not a very good picture, I'm afraid. Harrap Sinclair and Beadle.' I have reverted to the earlier reading in desperation. 'I can't imagine. How much?'

'Eighty-seven pounds.'

'Could it have been professional expenses?' I hazard.

'In connection with what?' My accountant is a patient and hopeful man.

'Perhaps I gave a party.'

'To some Americans?'

Inspiration suddenly returns. 'It was a carpet,' I tell him.

'A carpet in Weymouth?'

'Not exactly in Weymouth. Just outside. I bought a carpet for the drawing-room. I think we must call it private and not professional, although of course I do entertain on it at times. Americans too!'

I observe him hopefully, but he has alas already marked my carpet down as non-deductible. 'The Revenue,' he continues, 'is unwilling to concede that your trip to Paris in June '65 was solely and entirely for business purposes. They will allow a percentage of the flight costs and one night at the Ritz.'

But I am no longer listening. I am thinking of the magic carpet I bought at Weymouth and which was never really intended for the drawing-room at all. I came across it in a junk shop. I was convinced it was Persian and priceless. In point of fact it was British and worth about half what I had paid for it. Life is full of disappointments, full of accountants, full of financial crises, some people manage, some don't. It's as simple as that. All I know is that if I don't find a magic carpet pretty soon there is no hope at all.

Going Under . . .

The week my younger son passed his driving test and finally considered himself fledged, I paid a visit to my accountant and realised for the first time that I was featherless. What does an unemployed actor, in his sixties, partially deaf and weighing seventeen stone do when he discovers that he has thirty thousand pounds in the bank, and owes eighty thousand to the Inland Revenue? I shook hands all round, borrowed twenty-five pounds from my agent, and went and played roulette for an hour. It cheered me up, took me out of myself, cured my depression.

It's not the end of the road, though it is a familiar milestone. Bankruptcy figures in the index of a good many theatrical memoirs and when, as in my case, it is for a very considerable sum, it excites some of us and especially one particular colleague, almost to madness. 'How dare he!' he thunders. 'What is wrong with our tax system when it allows one man to owe fifty thousand and another to be hounded almost beyond endurance for seventeen pounds ten shillings?'

He will pose the question, but won't get an answer from me. All I know is that I have paid the Revenue roughly a quarter of a million pounds in Income and Surtax in my lifetime without ever being able to understand an Income Tax form, or to which particular year it refers. For thirty years my accountant has struggled to keep my head above water, swimming tirelessly by my side, turning me sometimes on my back and often gripping me in a vice-like frontal attack whilst striking me repeatedly on the chin lest I should panic and drown. Now, alas, his efforts unavailing, he must leave me to flounder. It is with great sadness that we part company, for although I have always been out of my depth, I have in a curious fashion enjoyed the bathe, indeed there have been moments when my feet seemed actually to touch bottom, and I believed in my ability to wade to the shore. But now I am finally and irrevocably adrift, no longer able or willing to fight the current, and only afloat because I am firmly wedged in the lifebelt of bankruptcy.

I am not sure as yet what being a bankrupt will entail. No doubt they will tell me. Do they, I wonder, give you a little individual pamphlet, or merely produce a large piece of cardboard with the instructions printed on it in bold type in the fashion of customs officials? How will it affect my wife, my children? It's idle to pretend that there won't be a slight feeling of embarrassment, even of shame. The actor always plays for sympathy, the comic exits singing a sentimental number to prove he is a good fellow at heart. No one ever suggested that he wasn't, any more than anyone suggested that a bankrupt is necessarily a crook, but from now on when I am recognised in the street, I suppose I shall not feel quite the same glow of satisfaction, or stop myself from wondering in which role I am remembered — the actor or the man who didn't pay up. They may even be wondering whether they too can manage to die owing the Revenue fifty thousand pounds.

How is it done? The first essential is to have accountants. It is not the slightest good going it on your own. Substantial tax arrears can only be achieved by a team. Provided the sum is substantial enough, and the point at issue of sufficient academic interest, there will be no lack of co-operation by the Revenue. There is nothing accountants or Income Tax Inspectors enjoy more than an appearance in front of the Commissioners. It is, after all, a day out for everyone.

There are two kinds of Commissioners, plain and fancy, or general and special, as they prefer to be known. I first appeared before the former in the late forties. I was startled to remark how many of them there were, and that they proposed, once having assembled to hear my case, not to pause for luncheon. My children were younger in those days and I had an appointment to escort one of them from Paddington Station to the dentist at one o'clock. In the end I was excused. Indeed, I think we even explained my problem to them in order that they might realise what a splendid father figure I cut, for an actor, of course.

When I returned, having dropped in for a snack at my club on my way back to the hearing, they were waiting to recall me to the witness stand.

'There is a question we should like to ask you,' said the Chairman, gazing at me intently. 'In the spring of forty-five/forty-six, did your children's nurse travel to the United States on an emigrant visa?'

I instantly realised this must be the sixty-four dollar question. I was anxious to answer truthfully. I was even more anxious to win for our side. I forget now which of the three possible answers I gave, but when shortly afterwards they returned a verdict in my favour, I invited my Counsel to congratulate me on my perspicacity. 'Things might have been very different,' I told him, 'if I hadn't answered that tricky question about the nurse's visa.' It was, he assured me, completely immaterial. 'Then why,' I asked, 'had the question been posed?' He shrugged his shoulders. 'Who knows?' he asked in his turn.

Winning the case cost quite a large sum of money, which everyone agreed was not deductible. For a long time afterwards the Revenue threatened to appeal, but when several months later they decided not to do so, everyone seemed to have lost interest. Besides, we were in that phase of my financial development which necessitated my becoming a limited company, and signing every contract twice over, in my dual capacity as actor and managing director of Robert Morley Productions Limited. I now had two sets of accountants, and a brand new office plate. All was peace and goodwill. I attended board meetings, signed minutes and cheques to the Inland Revenue as required, and if I wasn't entirely clear as to which years the sums related, I presumed everyone else was.

After about ten years the Revenue stirred again. It was, apparently, dissatisfied and wished to challenge the legitimacy of certain tax deductions which we had made. It invited me to select a year, any year, better still perhaps any two years on which a decision on principle could be made by the Special Commissioners. It took a considerable time before everyone was able to agree an opening date, but this time its performance lasted over a week, and the sixty-four dollar question was whether I considered myself justified in entertaining two of Her Majesty's judges in my dressing room at the Revenue's expense. It was not, of course, an everyday occurrence. In point of fact the judges only came once, and had a whisky and soda apiece, but it was the principle that fascinated Counsel and Commissioners alike.

There were other weighty points to decide, as, for instance, who was responsible for repairing a television set and whether a stage door-keeper wouldn't do just as good a job if he wasn't tipped by myself, acting of course on behalf of Her Majesty's Commissioners. At the end of the hearing, the Special Commissioners, of whom this time there were only three, regretted that the case had been brought by the Revenue, congratulated me as an honest man who had done his best to keep his accounts with the aid of two sets of accountants,

54

and found in my favour on all points but one. They added they hoped the matter would now be settled as soon as possible. Once again all that was settled were my costs, which as the case had lasted a week were a good deal heavier than last time, and still non-deductible.

The Revenue announced once more that it would appeal, but that was several years ago. For me the tragedy is, I suppose, that if anyone from the Inland Revenue had ever sat down across a table with me, found out how much I could afford to pay, and asked for a cheque, I would have so happily given them one, but they never did. Instead they bullied and frightened by demanding enormous, impossible amounts, and each time they were beaten back, waited and let the arrears pile up for the final kill. When I asked my accountant if anything could get me out of the mess I am in now, he thought for a long time, and I didn't care much for his answer. 'Yes,' he said. 'Death would help.'

But for me the band still plays here in my own country. It is better to stay and face the music for as long as it lasts. I have lived beyond my means. If the Revenue has anything to do with it, I suspect I shall not be allowed to die beyond them.

... Or Living Creditably

I am not fond of banks. They appeal to man's lowest instincts, terror and greed. I am always nervous in a bank, dreading the moment when the cashier moves away from the counter, clutching my cheque to consult a ledger, or just possibly the police. In my youth, when I was overdrawn, I was admonished in the tone of voice usually used to those whose flies are undone. Considering banks make their enormous profits out of the inability of their customers to balance their books, I feel all debtors with overdrafts should be constantly rewarded with flowers, chocolates, or at the very least a kindly pat on the head. My father was always threatening to horsewhip his bank manager, but there's not much of that spirit left around any more.

Now that the banks have finally been persuaded to publish their annual profits the cat is out of the bag. Not that I am surprised by the fortune they make by borrowing money at one percentage and lending it out another. Small wonder they can afford all the best sites and are constantly able, like the American Ambassador, to refurbish. Who pays for the hours of television and the acres of newsprint they employ to improve their image? I do. They should divide their profits not among their shareholders, but among their customers. Those of us who regularly maintain our overdrafts should get a few hundred at Christmas, and something substantial at Easter as well. Why shouldn't we share in some of the publicity handouts? How about my picture for a start, blown up in *The Times*? 'Mr. Morley who, when he has money, keeps it in our establishment, and when he hasn't, helps himself to what's in the kitty.' Does the public really believe that if the cupboard is bare they can keep a bank manager inside as a pet? I wouldn't be surprised. The public will believe anything. Soon we shall see advertisements for special foods to keep your bank manager in prime condition.

It was, if my memory serves me, and it seldom does nowadays, the

56

late lamented Martita Hunt who once years ago in New York was rung up by a friend, a banker of international repute, and asked to an early luncheon on the slopes of Manhattan. During the course of the meal, he quizzed her gaily as to her resources, enquiring which bank she favoured while in his city, and by the coffee had persuaded her as a personal favour to himself to withdraw her entire capital from some downtown branch and transfer it to a bank situated in the east eighties, whose manager was a personal friend, and would be so proud to have Miss Hunt as a client. On one point he was insistent, that the operation be carried out immediately, that very afternoon, and that she must withdraw her money in green-backs. 'It never does to transfer money from one bank to another except in cash,' he admonished her. 'Bankers are funny people, apt to get jealous,' whereupon he hailed a cab and sped her upon her way. Arrived at the bank, she found the process of withdrawing her savings took longer than she had expected, and it would be now too late to make the journey uptown with the loot. Cursing her friend the banker, she spent an uneasy evening guarding the treasure first in her dressing-room, then on the stage itself. When it was time for bed, she slept fitfully with the wodge under her pillow. In the morning she rose early and hurried to stash the bills away in safety, only to discover that it was a bank holiday. It was not a bank holiday in the strict sense of the word, just that some banks, and among them the one from which she had withdrawn her savings, had closed their doors forever. When she thanked the banker for his advice, he disclaimed all responsibility. He seemed to be unwilling to recall the luncheon conversation.

'To what, then,' she asked him, 'do I owe my good fortune?'

'Your timing, Madam,' he replied gallantly, 'impeccable as ever.'

When a film of my play *Edward, My Son* was being prepared, the producer insisted on a small advance party, in which I was mysteriously included, reconnoitring the terrain of merchant banking. As we processed from magnificence to magnificence I was struck by the fact that partners in a merchant bank never let each other out of sight for a moment. All business is transacted apparently not only under the same roof, but under the same ceiling, and within earshot of all.

'The one in the middle is the senior partner?' I asked the guide, as we paused to observe a pride of partners apparently slumbering after a kill.

'No, just the deafest,' he told me gravely.

I have planned for some time a treatise on the seven deadly

worries, paying particular attention to ways of increasing individual worry potentials. Money comes second in my list, immediately after health. Once a man has learnt to worry about these two, he can worry about anything. Most money worry begins at the bank, which is why we are seeing this vigorous new publicity drive to make the bank's image less alarming. All those pictures of mini-skirted girls who a few years ago were luring me to the seaside or the motor boat show now beckon me on towards the supreme folly of a deposit account. 'This is where the action is,' the message reads, 'in good old groovy Barclays or swinging Lloyds.' The scene, man, is the National Provincial. Fair enough, I suppose, if that's what attracts the customers and the bandits, but I'm not so happy when the appeal is to our children. I wouldn't want any of my children to believe that if they take care of the pennies, the pounds will take care of themselves. The pennies are for the small extravagances and the pleasures of childhood and for the nonsense of old age, for the poor of the neighbourhood, for the organ-grinder, for the fountain. Give your pennies away when you are young, or squander them if you wish. There is no happiness to compare with spending and giving, no sorrow to equal thrift.

My address, by the way, if you care to send a contribution, is Fairmans, Wargrave, Berkshire.

58

SARTORIAL
STUDIES

In Praise of Mr Robinson

It is not true that clothes mean nothing to me. When I was ten I sat sucking a straw on a stone wall and a child rode past in corduroy breeches and I was aware of sex for the first time, and for years afterwards haunted agricultural shows, bored to sobs, unless I could discover small girls in riding breeches, posting up and down on their ponies. Later I discovered in a shop in Monmouth a weekly magazine with a correspondence column of highly suspect letters, dealing with the dressing of little girls in breeches and hunted avidly for back numbers of the same paper, which did not continue to publish for long. There was a limited demand for such specialised fetishism. Nowadays, perhaps because my perversion seems slightly disreputable, I dislike the sight of little girls mounted on horseback, wearing those hard black hats and carrying whips. 'There's a streak of cruelty in that child,' I tell myself.

As for my own clothes, I have never taken kindly to them, although I am not of the stuff of which nudists are made. My own flesh burns rather than grills. I am seldom cooked to a turn. When I lie in the sun I take care to be fully clothed. I have a very old pocket watch which dreads the sand and for that reason I seldom venture onto the sea shore unless it is stony, and then only when fully shod and my watch well wrapped up in a handkerchief. People who lie for hours face down on the sand dunes should be removed by mechanical scoops.

My watch is the sole inanimate object to which I am attached. I care nothing for my pen, my cuff-links, my Pisarros. I once had a cigarette case of which I was moderately fond, but now I no longer smoke. Above all, I am not fond of my clothes. It gives me no pleasure to meet them every morning. I am bored by my under-clothes, irritated by the constant failure of the elastic in my underdrawers, dread the days when I have to walk round constantly hitching my waistline. I seem unable to foretell elastic fatigue. I am not attached to my handkerchiefs. When Cilla Black was a child she once waited for me outside the stage door, and begged a memento. I handed over my handkerchief and am still haunted whenever I meet her by the fear that it may not have been laundered at the time.

Only my ties occasionally give satisfaction, even a fleeting pleasure, but my favourites are always the first to become disfigured by gravy stains. I have learnt never to give my heart to a tie.

My shirts have to be custom tailored. I am too thick in the neck, too broad in the chest, for the fashionable rubbish on the ready-to-wear counter, where I sometimes glimpse a colour or a pattern which would favour me. 'Those are nice,' I tell them. Instantly, crushingly, comes the rebuke. 'Not your size.'

The real discrimination in the world is not between colour, but shape. I am segregated in New York, forced to shop at the outsize store next door to the Tall Girl Boutique. In the old days inns were obliged to provide food and lodging for the traveller, no matter how inconvenient or unprofitable such an exercise proved for mine host. Nowadays stores should be compelled to carry lines to accommodate the full figure. How insufferable are the advertisements for men's wear in the illustrated glossies, the bland assumption that the skinnies get the fat. How I loathe the arrogance of the well-groomed skeleton, stooping condescendingly to open the door of the sports car to decant the flashy bird. I even resent the horse in the background. I do not live in the world of cavalry twill. No dog nuzzles my legs if I can help it. Damn and blast all spindly-chested, unbuttocked men.

Years ago the discreet tailor enquired 'Which side do you dress?' I remember I was so taken aback I had to grope before I could answer. These days, men dress to the front. Before I die, we shall see the return of the codpiece and men will carry swords, if they're not doing so already.

What happened, I wonder, to all those elaborate trouser presses with the thumbscrews? At school, the prefects made the fags, as we were laughingly called, operate the contraptions. The expert among us could produce three or four different creases in the same pant leg, but were seldom thanked, except with a beating.

That habit of pulling the trouser slightly upwards with the thumb and forefinger as one sat, seems to have gone out of fashion, thank goodness. It always struck me as the height of economy. Not that I am extravagant where clothes are concerned. I buy my suits sparingly from a tailor to whom I was originally directed by Gabriel Pascal, who had engaged me to play Undershaft, the millionaire armament king in *Major Barbara,* and insisted that only Mr. Robinson, his personal cutter, could give him a run for his money.

Gabriel Pascal was a splendid, larger than life figure of a gypsy. His career was a superb confidence trick, although the confidence evaporated surprisingly on the studio floor, where he was perpetually bereft of his cool, and made me, at any rate, so nervous that I had to insist that once he had shouted 'Action!' he would leave the set – a procedure I have never been successful in adopting with any of my subsequent directors, though I once worked for one who kept a large packing case on the premises, into which he could creep and hide whenever I started to act. For the film, Pascal ordered and paid for a dozen suits, of which I wore at least three, and a black overcoat with a velvet collar which I still have thirty years later, but, alas, can no longer get into. A pity, as in the picture I only carried it over my arm. Rex Harrison, who played Cousins, was also directed to the same establishment, and wore his clothes with a good deal more panache. Later, when cast as a convict, he wisely insisted on Mr. Robinson cutting his prison garb. I once taxed the maestro with preferring to make clothes for Rex rather than myself, but surprisingly he was unenthusiastic about the pair of us. I could never understand what upset him about Harrison's figure, but I think I have presented him with a perpetual challenge. I suppose he has come to regard me with all the tolerance of a doctor for a chronic patient whom he manages to keep alive and reasonably active in the face of a crippling disease.

Mr. Robinson himself is now over eighty, but still stands all day in his establishment, ripping and pinning, and always careful to run every pin through his hair before inserting it into the cloth.

'Why do you do it?' I asked.

'I have forgotten,' he replied. I am reminded of the spot of carmine greasepaint I deposit in the inner corner of my eye when making up for a play. Some actors put carmine, too, on the ear lobes, but not I. There was a theory long ago and before Mrs. Patrick Campbell's devastating comparison of her leading man to a rocking horse, that one should also apply carmine to the nostrils.

Mr. Robinson, like myself, can be forgiven for forgetting. He started cutting, or at any rate devilling for a tailor before the turn of the century. He has a relish for the days when dukes drove up to his establishment in their dog carts, complete with tiger. 'You do know about tigers?' he said to me once. They weren't animals, but boys who sat on the back seat with folded arms and were as much a part

63

of the scene as the dalmatians who followed behind. When dukes arrived for their fittings, they would leap from the driving seat and race for the entrance, trying to reach it before the tiger had time to leap from the back and, flinging himself at the horse's head, strike the trusty steed on the back of the knee (or is it a fetlock?) so that he should stand properly. 'It was important how he stood,' Mr. Robinson assured me. Dukes apparently were intensely jealous of each other. They still are, as a matter of fact. In those days if they saw a carriage drawn by a better horse than their own, they couldn't wait to steal their rival's coachman. 'But surely,' I queried, 'it was the horse they coveted?' No. According to Mr. Robinson, the secret was always the coachman. I am reminded that Louis B. Mayer once wrote down for me in the order of importance, as he saw them, naturally, the qualities of a star. The ability to act came comparatively low on the list. Turn-out was all important.

'Here you are at eighty-two, still standing on your feet all day, while I am still a boy twenty years younger and get tired just sitting around. How do you do it?'

'You've named them,' said Mr. Robinson. 'You must have good feet, and know how to look after them.'

We were lunching at Buck's, a club started by my father-in-law, the late Herbert Buckmaster, to which I have belonged for many years, without making much impact. Mr. Robinson made an immediate impact. The members clustered at the centre table to listen. A good many of them, of course, are customers, who seldom catch him in a mood of relaxation. After luncheon I escorted my guest back to his premises around the corner, passing on the way a male boutique of alarming modernity and expense. I hoped that Mr. Robinson wouldn't notice the window, which displayed clerical collars in surprising colours and hair shirts complete with chains. 'I often go in there,' said Mr. Robinson, 'and give them my advice. They are young chaps, you know, just starting in the trade.'

There is a clue to my cutter. He is very loyal to his trade, although he does not subscribe to *The Tailor & Cutter* and refuses to exhibit at their annual exhibition. He has never won an Oscar. I once gave the Oscars, or at least their equivalents, away to the tailors, and if you think the Hollywood version is strange, you have no idea what sort of statues tailors cherish. Silver labradors, silver pheasants, miniature huntsmen pursuing miniature foxes across silver fences, silver chalices, silver beer mugs, silver stags grazing on nuggets of the stuff. 'Have you no gold?' I asked them. The ceremony was a lengthy one. There was an enormous list of prizewinners. All around the room were tailors' dummies, displaying the coat of the year, the waistcoat of the month. I made an impassioned speech, berating my hosts for their lack of adventure. I told them that their work on the whole was as dusty and fusty as their premises, and they were delighted. I told them they should petition the Queen to allow her subjects to dress informally for Ascot. I told them how unattractive I thought my countrymen looked in hired morning coats, and they clapped.

My speech gained great prominence in the trade papers, and three days later the Palace announced that men could wear lounge suits to watch the Ascot Gold Cup. But of course they didn't. I was the only one to avail myself of the privilege. Strolling around the lawns in my flannels and panama, I was annoyed by the number of people who peered at my name on the label which the Duke of Norfolk's lackeys pin to my chest on these occasions. Usually the start of recognition, the half-smile of delight suffices to put me in good humour, but on this occasion I was incensed by the fleet of elderly admirals, who kept reading my name as if for the first time, and looking at my clothes as if they had never seen a chalk pin-stripe before in their lives. *The Tailor & Cutter* offered me a suit, but Mr. Robinson refused to make it.

'I heard about you,' he told me, 'making a fool of yourself. Very bad for me.'

'How on earth,' I asked him, 'could it have been bad for you? I should have thought if your customers wore their own clothes to Ascot it would have put money in your pocket.'

'My customers,' he replied loftily, 'do wear their own clothes. It's only the actors who hire them. You don't understand the trade,' he went on. 'Why, there was a man came in here the other day who has a suit for every day of the month. Of course, he dresses for dinner every night, and naturally he has seven dinner jackets. But he was bored. "I look the same every night, Robinson!" he complained. He lives alone since his wife died. Won't come up to London, thinks it's dangerous. He could be right. He comes to Guildford. He lives just outside.'

'Mr. Getty?' I hazarded.

'Certainly not. I wouldn't dream of telling you the gentleman's name. Anyway, I solved his problem. I suggested cummerbunds, seven cummerbunds. He's as pleased as Punch, and different.'

Mr. Robinson demands a high standard of conduct in his fitting rooms. He has a particular horror of wives who accompany their menfolk to offer advice. When one of them confessed to a feeling of disappointment that her man still bulged in all the wrong places, and incautiously enquired if Mr. Robinson couldn't do something about it, he is said to have replied, 'Willingly, Madam, were I only a surgeon.' A duchess who complained that the waistcoat wrinkled when the duke sat down was invited to inspect his shirt, and forced to agree that that wrinkled as well, whereupon Mr. Robinson opened the garment. 'You will observe, Madam, that when he is seated, his grace's stomach is also prone to wrinkle.'

'What happens,' I asked Mr. Robinson, 'between the day I choose, or rather you choose the cloth, and the first fitting?' 'You wait,' he told me. On the other hand, if you are really in a fix or, in my case, a film, he will make you a suit in twenty-four hours without a fitting. He knows the rich like to be kept waiting, long to be rejected. My father-in-law was the same about his club. He would refuse people a table occasionally, even when there was room. 'They mustn't always have what they want,' he would remark.

In Mr. Robinson's and my father-in-law's world, people are children. 'I'll be with you in a minute,' Mr. Robinson says, and means 'sit down and wait quietly and don't make a fuss, that's a good boy'. We sit and wait and Mr. Robinson comes in with the jacket and waistcoat and puts them on a chair and goes away, and we are now in our underpants in a little cubicle, feeling as if we were going to have a medical examination, when the trouser cutter comes in. In all his long life, Mr. Robinson has never cut a pair of trousers, and wouldn't know where to start. The trouser cutter is quite unlike Mr. Robinson. He is not a star, and he is deferential. He has his jacket on, while Mr. Robinson is always in shirt sleeves. But perhaps the most marked difference is that the trouser cutter's trousers always fit perfectly at the first session. They are always quite perfect, and he is never surprised that it should be so. He leaves them on for Mr. Robinson to see, and we sit down again, waiting for the boss.

When he comes he surveys the trousers, but says nothing. He puts on the waistcoat, pins it roughly over the stomach, and enquires after my health. He removes the tape from around his neck, and measures my chest. 'Put on a bit, have I?' But Mr. Robinson in diagnosis doesn't answer the idle questions of his patients. It is just, but only just possible, that the fault is his. He puts on the jacket. It is not, of course, in a finished state. There are facings of canvas, a lack of buttons. The tape is produced once more, and this time worn by me briefly as a belt. Mr. Robinson pats the front. 'Very nice,' he says to no one in particular. 'Very nice.' The only parts that fit are the shoulders and the sleeves. Mr. Robinson pulls out a penknife, makes some deft incisions, gives a few swift tugs, and I am suddenly in my shirt again. Mr. Robinson calls out loudly for Albert. His name is echoed through the shop, as if we were in the corridors of justice, and Albert was a missing witness.

When he appears from the attic, or possibly the cellar, he is straight out of Galsworthy. His clothes are calculated to suggest immense deprivation. He is collarless. He gives me a humble smile of duty, touches his forelock and is instantly engaged by Mr. Robinson. 'I want you, Albert, to look at this revers. It wants taking up into the flèche. The shoulder will have to be lengthened.' The coat is now in pieces. The sleeves on the floor. All Albert's work — if it is his work, and I sometimes suspect that Albert is kept there as a whipping-boy and has no hand in the task — all Albert's work and Mr. Robinson's work is now destroyed, and you might think the pair of them would be down-hearted. But not a bit. They know that, unlike Humpty Dumpty, it will all soon be together again, only to be taken apart once more on my next visit.

Perfection will be achieved on the third and final occasion. Indeed, has already been achieved. The very appearance of a penknife at the third fitting is unthinkable. The coat fits, can be seen to fit and Albert is once again summoned, this time to be congratulated. 'I want you, Albert,' says Mr. Robinson, 'to see this for yourself. Very nice. Very nice indeed. And Mr. Morley, if he will forgive me saying so, is not an easy man to fit.' After I have thanked Albert comes the moment when Mr. Robinson ceremoniously adjusts the cheval mirror in order that I may admire the back. 'Just look at that back,' he urges. But I am not fond of the back. It is the moment of truth when I see how bald I am. Because my hair still grows in front and is there for me to brush every morning, I am always chagrined to observe in Mr. Robinson's cheval mirror that on top it doesn't grow at all.

Some years ago, visiting a mental hospital, I was introduced to a little old lady who was convinced that she was Queen Victoria, a monarch whom she closely resembled. Her condition was characterised by the medical staff as extremely disturbed, but she was calmness itself while receiving me in audience. I noticed that when she graciously dismissed me, Her Majesty spoke a few words in Welsh to the doctor who acted as her Chamberlain.

'What did Her Majesty say to you?' I asked him when we had withdrawn. He hesitated fractionally before replying.

'She wondered who the bald bugger was.'

'Bald bugger?' I repeated. 'Are you quite sure she said bald bugger? Surely from her height it must have been difficult to detect?'

I often wonder if those we think mad are not psychic into the bargain.

One thing about Mr. Robinson's suits is that they last forever. It is his habit to inscribe the date of each masterpiece on the label which he causes to be affixed to the right hand, inside pocket. It is always the same pocket, because that's how the police like it. Instant identification in the face of the untoward is a fringe benefit enjoyed by his customers. I am not a believer in the tradesman's right to stamp his name on the goods which he supplies. I don't really care for the name of my hatter on my hatband, nor am I remotely interested in the provenance, if that's the word, and I'm pretty sure it is, of my toothbrush. But I do not resent Mr. Robinson's intrusion. I am not a frugal or well-balanced man financially. I often puzzle over why Mr. Burton can afford so much, and I so little. But I like sometimes to remind myself that though in the debt of the Inland Revenue to an extent which neither of us exactly relishes, I am on the whole a sober citizen, and in such moments open my jacket and find reassurance by squinting downwards at Mr. Robinson's meticulous handwriting, to discover that the coat I am wearing was first buttoned by me in 1951, and what's more that I am still managing to button it.

The one outfit I have never purchased from my tailor, or worn, save in the pursuance of my trade, has been a tailcoat and the accompanying white tie and waistcoat. When still a comparatively young man, and appearing as Oscar Wilde in a play of that name on Broadway, I was asked to a supper party after the performance by the late Mrs. Cornelius Vanderbilt, who in those days still lived it up in her mansion on Fifth Avenue. I had already been to tea with her on several occasions among the roses, each in their separate silver vase, and the photographs of reigning monarchs and others who unlike Mrs. Vanderbilt had thrown up the sponge. But this was the first occasion on which I had been invited to a soirée. The dress, she indicated on the invitation, was to be formal.

'What would that entail?' I enquired of the social secretary.

'It means a white tie and tails.'

'I haven't got either, so I shall come in a dinner jacket and a black tie if that's all right.' I never dreamt for a moment that it wouldn't be. I was, after all, the toast of Broadway that season. Every taxi driver knew that my grosses were only topped by Raymond Massey impersonating Abraham Lincoln. Queer waiters used to thank me for what I was doing for them as they ushered me to the ringside seat at the Cotton Club. Walter Winchell had awarded me 'five orchids' and although his quote slightly interfered with my prominence on the playbill, this was heady wine.

On the morning of the party the social secretary rang back. It seemed that Mrs. Vanderbilt had been considering my problem, and thought it best if I were to come some other evening. I went to bed supperless, scarred for life, and vowing never to own a tailcoat. On the whole, my decision has been a wise one. It has caused me little inconvenience and has saved me a great deal of boredom. I have never wanted to conduct an orchestra, or play a cello. Moreover, I am reliably informed that men in white ties make even worse speeches than men in black ones.

The last time I was in Paris, emboldened by after luncheon brandy, I left the Ritz hotel and wandered 'lonely as a cloud' down the Rue Cambon and entered, in a moment of *folie de grandeur*, the Katharine Hepburn shop, or, as it is still known in Paris, Chanel's, and asked to see the collection. It was not the normal hour for viewing, or I believe the right time of the year, but I was told that if I cared to arrange myself they would do what they could. Presently, several lovelies appeared, wearing the little coats and skirts, the beaded cocktail dresses, the woollen evening gowns which are so instantly recognizable as Madame's handiwork, even by incognoscenti such as I. Halfway through the show, the brandy began to wear off, and I to be alarmed. How to get out, without buying anything? In that moment of panic, an idea for a story occurred to me — a hideous hunchback, or perhaps just a fat actor, enters the premises of a leading couturier and demands a fashion show. A frightened vendeuse accedes to his brutal request, whereupon he selects a dress on each of the models in turn, writes out a cheque and presents the delighted birds with their own feathers, gets into his carriage and drives silently away into the afternoon. On this occasion I simply got up and left before the bride put in an appearance. Maybe they hadn't planned to give me a bride anyway.

When it comes to collections, women still have all the fun. How pleased I would be if I found on one of my visits to Mr. Robinson, his sober premises transformed. The bolts of Harris tweed, the books of little square patterns banished, the pictures of drag hunts (no Freudian connotations here) and the portrait of the Japanese Emperor taken down. The leather armchairs replaced with rows and rows of the traditional small gilt chairs on which were seated merchant bankers, film producers, Venezuelan Ambassadors, Mr. Paul Getty, the Prince of Wales, even perhaps Mr. Hefner himself, watching 'the clothes of tomorrow worn by the men of today'. Down the staircase they would march, each one dressed to kill, in the bedroom, on the moors, perhaps on the battlefield itself, dressed to love, in the motor car or beside the swimming pool, dressed to dine at some glittering banquet, or merely to lounge elegantly, the tray on the lap, watching television. Dressed, in the final tableau of all, on this occasion only, on the arm of his bride, or perhaps, wiser to stick to his best man. We can't have women littering up the place. They will see the clothes later, and by the time we get round to such displays who knows, they may even be ready to pay for them.

For someone who doesn't enjoy dressing up, I have had my share in the fitting-rooms of the theatrical costumiers over the last forty years. I have stood patiently confronting the cheval mirror while a procession of wardrobe mistresses have tugged and sweated, have cut and pinned silks and satins, genuine ermine and synthetic chain mail to my resisting person. I have been laced into corsets and padded out with rubber foam. Even, on one occasion, fitted with angel wings. Always the perpetual struggle has gone on between the designer who tried to make me look different, and the actor determined to look much the same. In the end, of course, it is I who have triumphed and despite their efforts, all the great historical characters I have enacted, from Alexandre Dumas to Oscar Wilde, from W. S. Gilbert to Louis XVI, and from the Emperor of China to Prinny, have ended up looking extraordinarily like Robert Morley.

Only on one occasion has the disguise triumphed. In one of my very early professional engagements I was cast as Oedipus and prevailed upon to speak Greek tragedy through a sorbo-sponge mask. Understandably, my beautiful voice was muffled. An aunt who witnessed the débâcle summed it up forever as far as I was concerned.

'I didn't enjoy it much,' she told me. 'Do you know your mask looked as if it was made of sorbo-sponge?'

Tailor's Dummy

I was once hailed as one of the ten best-dressed men in the world. Like a fool I have lost the clipping which conveyed the joyful news and all I can state positively is that I came equal fifth with another national hero called George Best, that a tailor himself was top of the list and Lord Snowdon just scraped in as number ten. Mine is a remarkable achievement, as I have never before even entered the lists, and I cannot think why I haven't preserved the press cutting to add to my collection.

There wandered into my dressing room the other day the innocent grandson of a famous criminal lawyer with some notion of interesting me in a television series based on his granddad's more sensational *causes célèbres.*

'Do you know,' he told me, 'Grandfather actually kept a scrap book into which he stuck newspaper clippings about himself. He must have been a rather conceited sort of chap.'

'Very,' I told him gravely, and thought of my own bookcases bulging with the laudatory mentions earned by myself all those years ago in the *Wirral Advertiser,* and now preserved for ever in stout scrapbooks. I know few actors who do not follow my custom, but Q.C.s are made, it would seem, of more modest stuff.

I don't feel at all modest about being one of the ten best-dressed men. I am proud of having crashed the weight barrier, to have struck a blow for the properly-made man. I am heartily sick of those skinny ginks who figure in the advertisements, climbing in and out of shooting brakes with girls and dogs.

Years ago, when I went to the cinema and watched the Pathe Gazette cockerell, we were treated to seasonal fashion shows and after the wickedly seductive slinkies in cloche hats and silver fox, there came a glimpse of a stout matron who was, I believe, called Dorothy. Dorothy fashioned the more mature models for the more mature woman, never the bride or even the bridesmaid. She was that most revered of guests, the matron of honour, and I was always impatient to greet her from the one and three pennies. Dorothy always came up smiling, and I caught myself smiling back. It doesn't matter, she seemed to be saying, if one is no longer young, if one was never pretty. It doesn't matter if one is on the big side, indeed it helps.

On the big side, that's me, and I am proud to take my bow a little late in the proceedings, smiling bravely as I essay the catwalk and listen to the commentary. 'Here comes Robert in double-breasted blue flannel with just the faintest suggestion of a pin-stripe. Notice the outsize lapels, the slanted breast pocket with just the right amount of clean handkerchief displayed, the trousers cut generously to accentuate the *embonpoint* of the seat and the turn-ups kept wide to enable them to be pulled over the shoes. The coat is worn un-buttoned to give additional ease and avoid any appearance of strain. Thank you, Robert.' Thank you, Dorothy, if it comes to that. I wonder whether she still lives. Mr. Robinson, alas, is dead. All the years he cut my clothes he resisted the suggestion that I should include his name on the list of credits in the programme. Actors rather like to get an additional mention in the small print, along with Lux and Schweppes and the Post Office telephone. 'Mr. Morley is dressed by . . .' but alas, it was never to be.

'I'd much rather not,' he would tell me whenever I brought up the subject.

'Are you ashamed of me?' I once asked him.

'Not ashamed,' he replied, 'but then of course I'm not exactly proud either. It's not so much how you wear my clothes as the way you treat them. When you go to bed at night, why don't you hang them up?'

'I sometimes put them over a chair.'

'But mostly on the floor?'

'Mostly. Don't you think clothes like to be free occasionally, like pit ponies?' I asked him. 'It can't be good for them to spend their life on hangers. If you throw them around, they relax. That's my theory, anyway.'

'It's not mine,' Mr. Robinson told me.

Mr. Robinson took on all comers. I played Gilbert in a film of Gilbert and Sullivan. Osbert Lancaster, by no means an unintimidat-ing figure, was the designer and attended one of the fittings. Mr. Robinson surveyed his sketches with distaste and refused point blank to cut a slit for a watchchain in a tweed suit. When Lancaster eventually withdrew, Mr. Robinson bundled up the designs and gave them to me.

'If we're going to get on,' he remarked, 'we'd better get rid of these.' Then, unable to leave well alone, he shuffled through them resentfully once more. 'What I am wondering,' he observed, 'is whether this gentleman ever *saw* a morning coat.'

'Mr. Lancaster,' I told him, 'has always moved in the best circles.' But Mr. Robinson remained unconvinced.

I would have liked to have seen my old friend's face when I told him I had finally made the team, but it's too late now. There are some men in whose debt I shall always be proud to have been, and one of them is Mr. Robinson.

PEOPLE
AND
PROFILES

Dame Gladys Cooper

On the last evening of her life, my splendid and courageous mother-in-law, Gladys Cooper, rose from her bed and making her way, not without considerable effort, to her dressing-table, proceeded to brush her hair and make up her celebrated face. Then, gazing into the mirror for what was to prove the very last time, she remarked to her nurse, 'If this is what virus pneumonia does to one, I really don't think I shall bother to have it again.' She got back into bed and presently died in her sleep. Her looks were something she habitually shrugged off. People used to tell me, as no doubt they told her, that it was in her bones. 'If your bones are right, you can't go wrong. Look at Katharine Hepburn.' I go along with them to a certain extent, but believe that bones, just as clothes, must be worn with panache. A lot of women have good bones. Very few of them looked like Gladys.

Among all the letters the family received when she died was one from the secretary of The Postcard Club of Great Britain, assuring us that their historian had every card which featured Miss Cooper and that her beauty was thus preserved for posterity.

Most mornings of her life, Gladys received at least one letter returning one of these celebrated postcards. Occasionally they came in dozens, wrapped up in brown paper, announcing that they were from the collection of a deceased relative of the sender, and towards the end of her life she became increasingly suspicious of them. Like the late Maurice Utrillo, she would question their authenticity.

'I don't think that's me at all,' she would tell us. 'I'm sure there was another woman who used to pose as me at times.'

'But,' we would ask, 'who but you, dear, would dress up as a shepherdess and clutch a rake, a hoe and a besom while being photographed in Mr. Foulsham's or Mr. Banfield's back garden?'

Nothing would surprise me less than to hear that those two

gentlemen to whom my mother-in-law was in those days under exclusive contract, postcardwise, are alive and well and living in Leeds, producing that most favourite of all programmes, 'Stars on Sunday'. Anyone who has watched Anna Neagle or Louis Mountbatten undertake the chore, who has seen the choirs posed on on the Elizabethan staircase, James Mason reading the bible by the fire blazing on a hot summer day, must acknowledge how much the incongruity of the proceedings owe to these early pioneers of the absurd. Was it, I wonder, Mr. Banfield who worked the shutter and Mr. Foulsham who dreamed up the setting, or vice versa? Perhaps they collaborated in procuring the golf sticks and the tennis racquets, the artificial snowballs and the genuine dead trout. What was the significance of the teacup which so often appeared, half raised in salute? Was one of them perhaps a teetotaller? There was always something going on. Not a lot, perhaps, but something.

At times there was just the very faintest hint, the slightest trace of the erotic. One of my favourites shows Gladys with her hair in plaits and dressed in a brown peignoir over a pink wrap over a blue nightdress, about to open a bedroom door. But perhaps erotic is hardly the word. Saucy, that's what they were sometimes, saucy. When the children arrived and Gladys insisted on supplying these herself, life sobered up a good deal. Only the hats remained coquettish. There is one photograph of her sitting beside her first husband in a motorcar. She hadn't as yet taken the wheel, apparently. The expression is as always non-committal. 'Here I am,' she seems to be saying, 'what next?' And on this occasion of course, 'Where to?'

What did they do with all of these postcards, the great British public? And not only the British public. There must have been an enormous export market, hence the wording on the back: THIS IS A REAL PHOTOGRAPH OF A BRITISH BEAUTY. HAND-PAINTED ON RAJAH BROMIDE CARD. The insistence that the photographs were genuine gives a clue perhaps to the awe in which the sitter was held at any rate in later life. But who bought them, and for what purpose? Certainly not to send through the post. Very few of the ones in my collection are actually written on. The exceptions have a fascination all their own. 'As promised, here is the pretty baby. Those flowers you sent Mother were lovely. Things are in such an unsettled state I don't know when I wrote you. Haven't forgotten the headsquare, and shall send the prayerbook.' There is a sad little note from Geo. to Flo. 'I was watching for the post all day. Just a line hoping you are in the pink and still enjoying yourself.' At any rate nowadays the lovesick are put out of their misery a good deal quicker. Nothing in the morning delivery and you've had it, chum.

A good many of the cards were bought by soldiers in the last war but one to carry into battle. You couldn't be accused of being yellow if you put a thick wad of postcards in your breast pocket just over your heart. It was just that you happened to be a great womaniser and of course like everyone else, a fan.

To start life as a picture postcard and end as a Dame of the British Empire. After such a start it seems only natural that my mother-in-law's first job should have been in 'Bluebell in Fairyland'. Indeed about the whole of her early career in the theatre there seems an element of make-believe. The whole story of her success was almost too good to be true if she wasn't in a sort of fairyland, or at any rate a book written for children. This beautiful girl who went on the stage and in an incredibly short time became a star with all London at her feet. How it was done, the formula for this extravagant success, the lightning fame and fortune which in these days seems only to come to property developers, remains for me a mystery.

She never discussed past triumphs and when you asked her, all she would ever tell you was that she learnt her acting from Hawtrey. It was not that she was wilfully reticent, but when she recalled the past at all, it was to tell of the things that had amused her, the quirks of her managers, the practical jokes she used to play on her leading men. What leading men they were — Seymour Hicks, Hawtrey, Gerald Du Maurier, Ivor Novello, Owen Nares, and the one she married, Philip Merivale, and whose presence lived on in her life always, and whose family she adopted as she adopted us all.

Of all the performances I saw her give, my favourite was when she appeared in *The Indifferent Shepherd* and sat on the back of the sofa behind Francis Lister, or did he sit behind her? She had that unique gift of tugging at your heartstrings. Who can forget the curtain of *The Last of Mrs. Cheyney,* or her standing on the staircase in *Cynara,* or the curtain again of *The Letter?*

The pleasure of watching her on the stage before I ever dreamt I would be her son-in-law, and then the pleasure of being her son-in-law. Since she died I have thought about her often, always with a chuckle and always realising how much there was about her that I never found out. I never even discovered what she thought of me. I never even discovered if she knew towards the end of her life how ill she was. She had the most beautiful manners and about some things she never let on.

She could be very sharp at times. She was not good at feeling sorry for people, perhaps because she never felt sorry for herself. If you were in trouble, you got out of it, with her help of course, but it was up to you in the end. If you got ill, you got better. She was in her way something of a health fiend. She didn't eat much. She worshipped the sun. When we stayed with her in her Californian home she would come back from the studios at dusk and start cooking our dinner and then, when everything was in hand, she would disappear and a moment later sweep across the patio, wrapped in towelling, for her evening swim. Ten minutes later she would be back and five minutes after that she would reappear in the sort of shift dress of which she was so fond, gold bangles on her arms, her hair and her make-up immaculate, to mix a final round of daquiris before she took the lamb from the spit.

How is it done, I used to ask myself. How can she be so elegant? If she was vain about anything it was about her cooking. Two things you were never allowed to criticise — her marmalade and her driving. Both, I always felt privately, left a good deal to chance. But about everything else she was eminently reasonable. How good an actress she thought herself to be, how seriously she took her profession, I was never sure. She acted like she did everything else, naturally. But of one thing I am very certain. She was immensely proud of the affection and gratitude of her public. She answered every letter, she acknowledged every compliment and no day was too cold or too wet for her to pause as she came out of her stage door, or in later years the supermarket in Henley, to have a chat to a faithful patron who wished to compliment her on some past performance in the theatre or on the screen or on television, or on just being Gladys Cooper.

Laurence Olivier recalled her as hurdling the various fashions of the theatre, and if sometimes she knocked one over or it collapsed beneath her, she never faltered or shortened her stride. She raced ahead, and those who expected that one day she'd come back to her field were wrong. She was still in front at the finish.

Perhaps I've dwelt too much on her comparatively early triumphs, not mentioned her later ones, her films, but here again even the best of them didn't compare with the splendour and wonder of watching her in *The Bohemian Girl*. She loved television, was very proud of having done *The Rogues*. Asked once what she regretted in her life, she said, 'I was very sorry when *The Rogues* finished and when I just missed being the first woman to loop the loop. I was in the cockpit when the pilot's wife arrived, and I gave way. I didn't want to break up the marriage, but I've always regretted it. One should go on with things.'

She had a passion for all animals, the wilder the better. Ducks, cats, dogs, monkeys, parrots shared her houses with her, and she relished any opportunity of acting with lions or tigers or leopards or bears. Nothing scared her. Once on a beach at Acapulco a rifle bullet pinged past us. I turned and ran into the sea. Gladys turned and walked towards the firing. 'What happened to you, then?' she asked when I rejoined her. 'I had a sudden absurd desire to paddle. Was there a shot?' 'The gardener,' she told me. 'The owners of the house are away and he's been left in charge. Natural, really, he couldn't have been more than ten.' Natural, it's the word I most associate with Gladys herself; she was a natural woman.

Eric and Ernie

'We were wondering about the Burtons for our Christmas Show, what do you think?'

'Seventeen million viewers are not to be sneezed at. I should think they'd jump at it,' I murmured politely.

'Nineteen million,' Ernie corrected me.

'They need the money,' Eric observed.

Nineteen million viewers. I fell to working out how long it would take me to play to an audience of nineteen million, slogging along once-nightly in Shaftesbury Avenue, counting matinées, of course. I came up with various answers — ninety, fifty, seventy-five years, all approximate of course, and the theatre would have to be full every time, and people dissuaded from coming twice. A lifetime, that's what it was, a bloody lifetime, and Morecambe and Wise achieve it in one evening. I abandoned my attempts at mental arithmetic and found I hadn't been listening to a story one of them had been telling me about Billy Bennett.

We were rehearsing at the Kensal Green Community Youth Centre, sharing the building that afternoon with a Darby and Joan get-together. The territory was new to me, only Ernie's Rolls Royce parked at the entrance reassured. Years ago, the BBC surveyed the drill halls and Wesleyan Chapel premises for suitably austere quarters in which they could assemble the actors they were currently employing, and get them to do some serious rehearsing on the Corporation's behalf. They eschewed licensed premises and places within convenient reach of saloon bars, judging that under such circumstances, luncheon breaks were liable to be prolonged. In point of fact they have now reversed their dispersal policy and assemble most of their casts under one roof in Acton where, if there is no hint of overt festivity, chocolate biscuits and coffee can at least be purchased during certain well-defined hours.

The boys, as everyone calls them, however, prefer to remain put, far from the distractions of gracious canteen living and the patter of other comics. Even when you have been working with them, as I have been, it is sometimes difficult to remember which is which. 'The tall one has the longer name. Remember that, and you can't go wrong,' the producer told me, but then it's Ernie and Eric that cause the confusion. For most of the morning and afternoon, come to that, they tend to sit round a table, reading their lines from atrociously-mimeographed copies of the script. Once in a while one of the assistants will rearrange the chairs to indicate the tomb of Tutankhamun, our present project, and everyone gets up, still holding the script, and shuffles round while the director plays the part of the camera. It is by no means an exact science. Years of the music halls have made it almost impossible for them to give anything but impromptu performances. Lines are added, subtracted, rearranged. There is no indication of the final draft. Towards their guests they adopt a protective solicitude. They realise you will never really learn to swim in their tank, but they are insistent that you should have your share of the ants' eggs. Are they happy in their bowl? The answer must be yes. As Victor Borge once said to me, 'It's wonderful when the cream comes.'

Sometimes, and for no very apparent reason, they will go off and open a store in Morecambe or Preston. When they do, the town they have selected stops for the day. Ten thousand people line the streets.

'Of course,' says Ernie, 'we could do the whole thing in ten minutes, but it takes forever. There's all the palaver when we are introduced to the directors' wives over coffee and biscuits, and then the Mayor arrives and we move on to the sherry, and then finally we move on to the store. And then of course there's luncheon afterwards. It takes the day.'

'Why do it?' I asked.

'We do it for the money,' they tell me, but of course they don't. They do it because they feel an obligation. Exactly to whom, they would be hard-pressed to tell you, certainly not to the proprietors of the store. Perhaps to the very first rubberneck who arrives that morning outside the shop, prepared to wait for three or four hours for Ernie to cut the ribbon and Eric to make a joke, simply because in this forward-looking society of ours, he has absolutely nothing better to do.

At half past one on the first afternoon, Ernie unpacked some sandwiches from a plastic bag and accepted a cup of coffee.

'We don't usually stop for lunch,' Eric explained.

'I do,' I told them, 'Is there a pub nearby?'

'Not for miles.' In the end, Eric gave me half his sandwiches and an apple. Next day I ordered lunch in picnic boxes from Fortnum's and handed them round. After that, the boys brought champagne and lobster. For a week we lived it up. One day Eric lent me *his* Rolls to drive back to Piccadilly, on another I walked. I had no idea how long the Portobello Road was, or how strange. I walked past shops boarded up and covered with protest slogans about the police, shops which gave clothes away. I walked into a betting shop and a huge Jamaican invited me to stake him on the four o'clock.

'What do you do?' I asked him, idiotically.

'Nothing,' he told me, 'I don't do nothing, just gamble.'

I am a nervous man. I refused him and walked out, looking back over my shoulder, asking myself whether here in London in the middle of the afternoon in the middle of the Portobello Road, I was safe.

I never feel safe somehow in the Television Centre. It's not that I haven't done my homework, but that I am too nervous to remember it. If you don't do and say exactly what you've been taught, they can't cut the thing properly. After the dress rehearsal, I wandered away in search of a cup of tea. Television Centre is designed as a maze. You can go round forever in circles. I kept meeting foreigners in the long dark passages and being misdirected. Finally I ended up on the sixth floor outside a room marked Chairman. Dare I enter? 'I was wondering if there was such a thing as a cup of tea about?' I tried the handle, but it was locked. Eventually, I found a hot cross bun and munched it behind a door which was marked Cameramen Hospitality, one of the few rooms in the building to have a window, and I looked down on London from a great height and told myself to stop worrying. What does it matter, I asked, supposing I don't get it right?

But to Eric Morecambe and Ernie Wise it matters a great deal. Aloft, and determined to stay in orbit, they leave nothing to chance until splashdown. Then, their mission completed for another week, they fish the champagne bottles out of the bath in dressing-room 1517, and pour it for their guests.

Dr Issels

I am not fond of the Germans and I admit my prejudice. When I was a student in Hanover lodging with a minor bank official, I was depressed by the unearthly hours he kept. I distrust early risers. A man who gets up before me wants to get ahead of me, and the Germans always wanted to get ahead of everyone, and still do.

They have a matchless enthusiasm for the efficient and impersonal approach. If it works, it is good enough for them. If a German works he is good enough for anyone, no matter at what he works. I detected a hint of pride in the taxi driver's voice when he pointed out Himmler's one-time villa — farther up the valley and across the lake was where Goebbels used to lodge.

The Bavarian Christmas trees were covered in snow, the Bavarian motorways were swept clean and the taxi was a Mercedes Benz. We were on our way to the Ringberg Clinic, much in the news these days, where Dr. Issels engages his mortal enemy. I have a friend with terminal cancer and a corner in the ring, and Issels is with him night and day urging him forward, comforting, cajoling, willing him to continue the fight, insisting that he will win.

Every now and then I take a plane to Munich and drive the fifty odd miles to Rottach Eigern, putting up at one of the huge empty hotels on the little lake; and having left my bag in the empty bedroom with the bare white walls and the hideous pine panelling and the soapless bathroom, put on my galoshes and trudge up the road a few hundred yards to where my friend awaits me.

Once he surprised me by the porter's desk just as I was delivering up my key. When he left England he was in a wheelchair but on this occasion he strode toward me, almost as he used to do. The doctor had observed him using a walking-stick the day before, and took it from him. 'Don't walk like an old man. Why do you walk like an old man?' No one knew the effort it had cost him to walk those few hundred yards, but he did it because he thought that, when he heard, Issels would be pleased with him.

Issels hears everything. He is the wind that blows along every corridor — a short, stocky, middle-aged professor in a white smock, he constantly patrols the camp — half a dozen small villas and one larger central block, still small by hospital standards. They say a grateful patient paid for the new laboratories and the kitchens. The food is unlike the food the patients eat at home — there is no attempt to reproduce tepid cottage pie and soggy sprouts. The food is cranky, usually vegetarian in tone. There are curious fruit purées and molasses; there are things that have to be mixed with other things; there is cheese but no butter; there is an occasional glass of what is called natural wine. My friend finds it appetising and knows, or seems to know, the order in which each dish should be consumed. It is the sort of food one might find on a Japanese health farm.

My friend's day is lived as if in a gymnasium. He trains and fights, recovers from the contest and trains again. It is Issels who decides the days when he punches the bag, the day when he walks the road, the day he must go into the ring and engage his opponent. On these latter days he is given a very high fever and a thermometer, and as the mercury rises or falls he must trace its progress on a chart. He must know even when his teeth are chattering and his knees knocking and his head swimming. He must know what he is about. Issels is there in his corner all the time, but only at the end of the fight will he examine his chart to see how he has fared, and holding his hand, speak soft words of congratulation.

He is a great showman, Issels, but he is also a genuine giant, and for his patients he is something more — he is Hope. Their only hope, and they come to him from all over the world. They hear his name on the television, they read it in the newspapers, or his Clinic casually mentioned by a friend. That is enough. They pack their bags, they load the caravans, they bundle up the children and they arrive on the doorstep.

In the room next to my friend is the wife of a Greek shipping-millionaire. The entire family seems to live in the corridor outside. There are brother and sisters, and an aunt and the Primate of the Greek Church, but I fancy he and the priest who accompanied him are on a briefer visit.

Next door is an Englishman who used to drive an oil tanker — the vehicle developed an alarming swerve. He drove it for a week complaining of the steering every time he returned to the garage, and each time it was checked and pronounced in perfect order. Then, getting out of the cab one evening he fell down and found the fault. He has cancer of the brain. His wife feeds him every half hour through a tube. They have no visitors. The children are home with the grandparents and fretting. Issels is not pleased with the way in which the charts are kept by the wife but she believes he will cure her husband. 'He knows what is wrong with him — never mind the charts. I reckon that's just to keep me occupied to stop me from worrying.'

In the children's ward there is a huge picture window and the mothers take the children on their laps and sit watching the snow. It's a sort of Disney Land — 'ever so pretty' — one of them says. The children are the only ones Issels does not tell. Their parents take the temperatures and sit holding the glass with the straw. They get through a lot of straws. I am reminded of a holiday camp when the weather is bad and these parents, like all parents, are determined to make the best of it. There is a little girl who may be allowed out of bed in three weeks if the X-rays prove satisfactory. Her father is confident she will walk again. She has a ring on her finger and I ask her if she is married. She shakes her head. I ask her if I might see her ring and she takes it off and hands it to me. I notice that someone has attached a rubber band to the back.

'We had to do that otherwise it would fall off now,' says her father, cheerfully.

The child produces a tape recorder. 'Why don't you say something?'

Idiotically, because I can think of nothing else, I start to recite 'If'. When I get to the bit about . . . 'if you can force the heart and nerve and sinew to serve their turn long after . . .' I stop abruptly. 'I'm afraid I've dried up,' I tell her.

When I said goodbye to my friend on my last visit, I asked him if he felt like coming home, giving up the fight not altogether, of course, but for a little time for a breathing spell. I thought he might be happier in his own home, not so far from his friends. I thought perhaps he deserved a rest from his dreadful battle. He shook his head. 'I shall stay here,' he told me, 'Here at least I have a chance. More important, perhaps I'm giving Issels his chance. You know what I like about Issels best? He hates cancer.' My friend's voice has got much softer lately, but the last three words were shouted in my ear.

I don't know whether Issels has found a cure for cancer — probably not — but I think the Herr Doktor deserves his patients, and that is the highest tribute I can pay them both.

TRAVELLING
HOPEFULLY

Traveller or Tourist?

I was five years old when I volunteered to stooge at a Christmas party for the local conjuror. 'What a nice little chap,' he said, taking me on his knee. 'But I think he needs oiling.' He produced a mammoth oilcan, and threatened me with it. I screamed and screamed and screamed and screamed. Never again have I screamed so loudly or so continuously. The conjuring show had to be abandoned, then the party. I screamed all the way home, and when they were putting me to bed. I screamed in my sleep for several nights to come. Was I, I ask myself, a normal child? Certainly. I have a natural horror of stooging.

The tourist is the perpetual stooge. There is no occupation which offers him more opportunity to humiliate or to make a fool of himself. The assumption is there almost before a man buys a ticket to travel. By the time he reaches the airport, the process is in full swing.

Most airports, and certainly all European ones, have been built and are still operated as cattle markets. How long will it be before mankind is actually marshalled to the plane by dogs, each country patriotically displaying its preference? Heathrow could have its bulldogs, slobbering and waddling threateningly behind us; Paris, poodles, snapping at our heels; alsatians crouching, menacing us at Munich. In New York, a pack of various breeds, hunting us down the endless tunnels. In a successful attempt to break the tourist's spirit long before he is airborne, the authorities have devised their fiendish drill. The loud-speaker system, adjusted every morning by skilled engineers so that they can only just not be heard, blare their instructions. One enquires nervously of one's neighbour whether he has received the message. 'Loud,' he replies, 'but not clear. I think passengers for Moscow on Flight SUR 950 should proceed to Gate 12 for immediate embarkation.'

Now ensues the customary tug of war with my nerves, already stretched to breaking point for fear of a last moment Customs swoop and the discovery of an illegal £7 15s in my trouser pocket. I know if I comply I shall find myself all too soon tightly wedged on a loading ramp, exits to which are secured and guarded by young women of ferocious mien, whose regulation costumes include an Edwardian motor veil knotted tightly under their assertive chins. They will make no effort to open the gates for at least another ten minutes. There is little point in their so doing. The bus which is to convey us to the plane is still in limbo. The arms of my fellow passengers are beginning to throb painfully under the weight of the personal luggage they have planned to cheat aboard. Shall I humiliate myself by joining the mêlée? Dare I wait, and risk being left behind? I durstn't. When I arrive to take my place in the block, the wardress is on the phone. She invariably chooses this hour to call her date for the evening ahead. Eventually the gates open, the bus arrives, and the passengers surge towards it. If anything could be less attractive than the behaviour of the ground staff, it is that of the passengers themselves. Each is determined to secure a favourable place on the plane, and just sufficiently cunning to realise this can only be achieved by being first off the bus. They stand as near the door as possible, refusing to move along and make it possible for those who follow to enter. Finally everyone is aboard save the one indispensable, the bus driver himself. When he puts in an appearance, and drags us away, the expression on his face mirrors the contempt he rightly feels for so craven a load.

Released from the bus eventually, but not before the wardress gives the word of command, we push and fumble each other up the steps, prise ourselves into miniature seats, and if they are long enough, which in my case they seldom seem to be, adjust our seatbelts and wait for the air hostess's insincere and improbable welcome. Why, oh why do we have to be told the name of the Captain? — surely a matter of supreme indifference to us all. In the long history of rail travel, in which far more was achieved in the direction of passenger comfort, it was never thought necessary to acquaint all and sundry with the identity of the engine driver. The credibility gap between airline advertisements and airline performance has a growth rate which must be the envy of all economic experts. It isn't only that the food is of increasingly poor quality and that there is less and less room to eat it; that the air hostesses become increasingly ungracious and the lavatories smaller and fewer in relation to the passenger load, it is that we tourists, by being so craven, cowardly and supine, have brought it all on ourselves.

One Steppe at a Time

Over the years I have always extolled the Soviet; in countless arguments across countless dinner tables I have defended the Communist way of life. Believing the Tsars to be monsters of wickedness, I must of necessity champion those who overcame them. To me the issue was simple; it always is. Besides, I delight in talking about matters of which I know nothing. Always at some stage of the row, and having infuriated my opponents, they would ask if I had ever been to Moscow, and always I told them I had. Even if I was troubled by the lie on the first few occasions, I eventually came to believe it myself. The other day, seeking new pastures to explore, I attempted a visit to China, but was repulsed on the doorstep of the Consulate. 'Why not try Russia?' I asked myself. 'I've been to Russia,' I replied. 'No, you haven't,' I was told, and straight away went round to Intourist. The lady at the desk was my sort, affable and rotund.

'How will I manage for money?' I asked.

'You are an artist,' she told me. 'You will do an artistic wangle.'

From that moment I knew I should enjoy the Russians. But Russia is by no means the Utopia I have always claimed it to be. There are times when one finds oneself in a land dreamed up by Lewis Carroll and decorated by Emmett. The regime is defeated by the weight of numbers. Everything looks as if it would function perfectly until you add the customers. Nothing, in the final analysis, is equal to their insatiable demand. Everything is in short supply at one time or another, except the queues. The art of shopping must be to arrive at the precise moment when the goods turn up, and before the crowds gather. Standing idly in a department store beside an empty counter, I could, had I wished, have purchased a live carp which chose that exact moment to arrive, in company with hundreds of its fellows, in a huge tank which was suddenly wheeled forward. Like lightning a

93

queue formed, and for once I was at the head of it. Splendid Russian ladies, their hands heavily bandaged — presumably from former fish bites — seized the carp and thrust them, still threshing wildly, into paper bags, weighed them and then handed a ticket to the lucky purchaser, who beetled off to queue by the cash desk, and then to descend once more to claim her prize, giving the ticket to the girl, and the carp a smart rap over the forehead to make it easier to carry away. If you found yourself at the end of the queue, the whole operation might have taken you half an hour, by which time of course the carp line might have snapped.

There are now very few Hotel Metropoles left in the world, but Moscow is still stuck with hers. It was the first hotel to which I was assigned in Russia, and far and away the most uncomfortable. A bedroom on the fifth floor, furnished with shabby simplicity, a dripping lavatory pan, and of the two lifts by which it could be reached, only one ever in service, and that usually stuck between the landings.

In the enormous dining-room every third light flickered in the chandeliers, and I encountered for the first time the Russian waiter's habitual determination not to serve his customer as long as he can avoid doing so. Until one grows accustomed to it, the hostility alarms. He will watch you alight at his table with smouldering fury in his eyes, and then with a violent wave of his hand, indicate that you are to take yourself off. I was reminded of bird scarers in Ceylon. If one is cowardly enough to move to another perch it will only be to encounter the same peremptory dismissal from another custodian. It is better just to sit it out. Once having decided he is not going to shift you merely by gestures, the waiter will adopt other tactics. Employing the technique of Russian schoolteachers in dealing with a recalcitrant, he will try to convince you that you do not exist. Passing rapidly by your table, he will stare through you at the wall beyond, and should you attempt to attract his attention, will studiously ignore your signal. However, after about ten minutes or so, there will be a sudden change of tactics. He is beside you, with a menu, even possibly a napkin, a knife, fork and a glass, and from now on it's just a question of time. He will continue to pass by your table on his way to and from the kitchens, once again ignoring your presence, and spending interminable periods behind the scenes; but now, in some curious way, your roles are reversed. He has become the bird and in time, with inordinate patience, and by remaining absolutely motionless, you will give him the courage to alight once more beside you, and this time take your order.

The traveller does well to remember at this stage that most

Russian menus are pure fantasy. Whether such dishes as baked hazel grouse or sturgeon roasted in silver paper ever actually existed, even in the days of the late Tsar, must surely be doubted, but they remain stubbornly on the menu, a constant trap for the unwary, and should one be tempted to order anything of this exotic nature, the waiter will instantly withdraw, without even bothering to write down such a flight of fancy, returning from the kitchen in due course, beaming with pride and happiness, to pronounce the magic word 'Niet'. The choice thereafter is almost invariably between boeuf Stroganoff, chicken Kiev or hamburger, and it is always a mistake to order borsch, or indeed a first course of any kind, as the waiter, now understandably exhausted and eager to close the joint, will bring all the dishes at once in order to get the whole painful business finished as soon as possible, and while you swallow your soup, the rest of the food congeals. Occasionally the traveller will find a restaurant at which he will be made almost welcome. In Samarkand I had a table fetched from the kitchen, and a place on it laid up for me, but such happenings are rare indeed.

I am not much of a one for museums, but not to have visited the Kremlin would have been unthinkable. I toured it in three hours, a good deal of the time panting to keep up with the guide for fear of becoming attached to one of the other delegations who, like us, scurried through throne-rooms and up and down staircases leading to Chapels and Water Towers, and of course more throne-rooms. How the Tsars would have hated us all, and how right they would have been to do so. For one thing we are far too many, and for another we look so apathetic. We must of necessity ration our rapture. We cannot swoon with ecstasy for fear of falling behind. Confronted with one showcase, we are forever asking ourselves what the next one holds. Inspecting eight Gauguins on one wall, we look around for the other four listed in the guide book. We are children opening the presents, but alas, we shall never have time to play with the toys or even, perhaps some of us, to see them again.

The treasures of all the Tsars, displayed before my popping eyes, consisted almost entirely of enormous gold platters. I don't see how anyone could have got most of them through a door, let alone on to a table, but the enthusiasm of the Russian rulers for such objects appears to have been unbounded. They were constantly receiving them from, or dispatching them to, their favourite relatives, or relative favourites. There was also a collection of coaches, and a golden train constructed by Fabergé to run round the Imperial nursery carpet on little golden rails, and to be wound up with a little golden key. The Romanovs were fond of gold — a family of magpies who suffered the fate of vermin with unwonted dignity.

Back in Red Square, we joined the crowds waiting to watch the changing of the guard. As the clock strikes the hour, the two soldiers on either side of Lenin's tomb are relieved in a curiously unnerving ceremony. The sentries, motionless as the corpse they guard, are replaced by two more of the elite in a manoevre so swift that the eye can scarcely follow it. Still not certain, indeed, whether they had actually changed places with their comrades, I watched them march off in solemn goose-step, commanded by a single officer, and finally disappear into the fortress. The crowd dispersed, in so far as the crowd ever disperses in Moscow.

The magnet to which all Russia is drawn, where all decisions are taken, the centre of the web, the seat of power, is in fact a hideously overcrowded provincial town. Without the beauty of Leningrad, the charm of Samarkand, the excitement of Siberia, there is little to catch the eye or enthuse the senses, once you have visited the Cathedral of Saint Basil and admired the Gauguins in the museum. Across the river, next to the largest open-air heated swimming pool in the world, is the permanent exhibition of Soviet achievement, containing all the enormous triumphal arches, golden fountains and outsize space rockets you would ever want to see. In vast farm buildings, enormous white bulls, huge pigs and the celebrated caracul sheep from Bukhara, bedded on wood shavings, their immaculate coats shampooed and curled, wait patiently for inspection, their stillness as unnatural as that of the sentries.

Most curious of all the phenomena in Moscow is the celebrated subway, the platforms of each station seemingly designed for a State reception. The one through which I was conducted happened to be decorated in the style of Louis XVI, the marble floors reflecting the glitter of a hundred chandeliers hanging from the ceiling, and here all the bulbs were for once alight. Was it possible, I asked myself, that the engine driver might be arrayed in white breeches with silver buckles on his shoes and a full-bottomed wig? But alas, when the train drew in I caught ne'er a glimpse of him, so great was the crush and so intense the struggle to climb aboard. Versailles was never like this, I reflected, as I made my way up the escalator and back into the street where, in the rain, a long queue waited patiently to buy matches. Whoever built Moscow subway had a great sense of humour.

Russia was full of water melons at the time. Though one doesn't see them much in the hotels, there seems a brisk demand for them at

96

most street corners. Like ice-cream and some vegetables, these are sold on the free market. There are no supermarkets and as most shops specialise in one line of goods, it seems as if the housewife is kept pretty much on her toes, which is perhaps the reason why, although they are mostly about my weight, they are so incredibly spry. Even when they are quite elderly, the Russian women never seem to let up. An army of grandmothers and great-grandmothers are out in all weathers, sweeping the streets. They are warmly clad, immensely cheerful and apparently undaunted by the task of collecting the leaves as they fall, and carrying them away in small tin cannisters, and when the trees are bare there will be the snow.

As we ventured forth one evening on our way to see *My Fair Lady* at the Theatre, we came across a group of them sitting on a little bench under the plane trees. They were laughing and chattering to each other as if it was the pleasantest thing in the world to be sitting in the dusk in the cold and the rain, and waiting for Heaven knows what. More leaves to fall? Perhaps a bus to take them home to their fire-sides and their grandchildren? The trouble, one Russian explained to me, is that the old ladies are allowed to earn money on the side, besides drawing their pensions. Most of them prefer to sweep up the leaves than stay at home with the grandchildren — for one thing it's more profitable, and oddly enough they find it more amusing.

I do not understand the Russians, but then I'm not particularly anxious to do so. Admire them? That's a different matter altogether. It's easy to do that, especially perhaps in Leningrad, where through the centuries in countless struggles against tyranny they have suffered and died and prevailed. There is hardly a square in this most beautiful city without a statue commemorating some outrage against the citizens. Here they were mowed down by the Cossacks, there hanged by the Tsars, everywhere they were burnt alive by German bombs. For three years they endured the worst that Hitler's armies could do to them. In one year Nature herself took a hand. It was, they will tell you, as though she wanted to test us too. But they fought on, with the temperature forty degrees below freezing, with no heating or light, no water, no transport. They carried their relatives to communal graves and died on the way home, and when spring came, men, women and children volunteered for three hours every day to clear the streets of the dead bodies, and thus avert an epidemic which might have finally conquered them.

They ate glue and sawdust, but they never thought of surrendering. In Leningrad, where the revolution was born, it was a possibility not to be contemplated.

They have been forged in tremendous fires, and they have emerged triumphant, but what sort of people are they? Yesterday, because I was pushed for time and because to eat in a restaurant cannot be done under an hour, I resorted to the hotel cafeteria, and snatching my coffee and cakes, and finding all the chairs occupied, went and sat on a staircase. An old gentleman, coming upon me unexpectedly, was plainly horrified. He lectured me on the impropriety of my conduct, but I was determined to misunderstand him until I had finished my doughnut, then smiling and waving gaily, I returned to the counter for more coffee (the coffee in Russia is unvarying in its excellence). This time the lady serving me and the gentleman who had chided me, led me firmly over to a now vacant chair. The war, the struggle, was over, they seemed to be saying. Now for Heaven's sake let us all try to behave like civilised people.

The Trans-Siberian Express

I arrived in Irkutsk, the capital of Siberia, in two minds as to whether or not to pick up the Trans-Siberian Railway, or to drop the idea once and for all, and fly the rest of the way to Khabarovsk. For one thing, Intourist had given me a plane ticket instead of the rail one I had requested, but whether by accident or design I couldn't decide. For another, my friend the Flying Dutchman, whom I met earlier in Bukhara, had painted for me a gruesome picture of the jollity on the train. Drunken Russians climbing in and out at every station; enormous ladies being hoisted up onto the upper bunks and falling back on top of everyone; the smell of the food, the state of the lavatories, above all the incessant singing of the peasants. Admittedly I was only joining the train at the halfway stage, but it still left three days and nights of a rugged community life in which, so my friend assured me, I should really get to know the Russians. But did I want to?

It was the food that finally decided me. For some reason, all the Irkutsk restaurants seemed permanently reserved for private receptions; munching salami in a bar, I was harangued by a Russian soldier. 'He is trying to tell you,' a bystander explained helpfully, 'that he has a brother in Vietnam.' 'Tell him,' I replied, 'that I have an aunt in Czechoslovakia,' and drifted rapidly towards the door before he could get the message.

The next morning I caught the train, and found myself sharing a compartment with a retired fruit farmer from Adelaide, who drank nothing on the journey, and sang hardly at all. The sun was shining, the air as balmy as Bournemouth. The guide was almost affectionate when she saw me off. 'Shall I need snowboots when I come to England?' she asked. A lady came and made up the beds, hoovered the compartment and brought tea. In the restaurant there was champagne and caviare. All day we hugged the shore of Lake Baikal.

On the great plains, Russian cowboys and cowgirls in quilted dressing gowns herded the cattle. We stopped at little towns where for once there were no great blocks of workers' flats and the houses were built of wood. The children were skating or pushing themselves across the ice on sleds. On the platforms there were stalls selling preserved fruit in jam jars, and tripe in paper bags.

In the evening about seven, we are invaded by a Russian officer, his wife and daughter, not pleased to find they have to occupy separate compartments. If I surrendered my bunk there would be room for them, but my instinct of gallantry soon passes. He speaks only a little German. He thinks East Berlin is a fine city. In reply to my query as to whether Russia and Germany are now friends, he flings up his hands. 'How about the Chinese?' He laughs and shrugs. I get the idea he is going to Vietnam, and am resigned to having him with us for the rest of the journey, but in the morning he is gone. I wash in cold water. More of a lick and a promise, as my mother was always saying. How it used to annoy me, along with her other adage 'It is necessary that a door should be open or shut.' Mother always said this in French. Now, in the middle of Siberia, with a slight anxiety that I may have jammed the lavatory door and will have to stay until I am released, I find it comforting. I wonder whether my children will remember my reiterations with affectionate irritation. What are my pet sayings? I rattle the door again, and this time it gives. It was, after all, with mother that I saw *Shanghai Express* and longed ever afterwards to come on this train. But now, alas, there are no Chinese prostitutes, no bandits disguised as Russian officers, no Marlene Dietrich, no Anna May Wong, no Warner Oland, no suave Englishmen, only myself and a few Australian tourists.

What a poltroon I am, this constant anxiety that I shall lose my passport, or get left behind at the station. What would happen? Presumably one wouldn't be eaten. Still, on the platform I never take my eye off the guard, and am always the first to climb aboard. Siberia is looking a trifle more rugged. We manage to clean the windows. The radio from the next compartment blares a constant exhortation. Why am I so sure it's not just a cookery lesson?

For the rest of the journey we have the compartment to ourselves. My companion reads nothing but a travel guide to the hotels in Japan and pores over his itinerary. When he talks it is of remembering to retrieve his ticket, which he surrendered to the lady with the hoover. On the fourth day we are woken at five, and alight at Khabarovsk. Here the Trans-Siberian Express disembarks its casual passengers, and continues to the great submarine base at Vladivostok. For tourists this region is out of bounds, and they are funnelled down a shute to Nakhodka. The journey is made overnight in Russia's most up-to-date train — wide, comfortable beds, private bathrooms, and something that has been missing from our journey from Moscow — hot water.

The train had hardly started, when the Devil, in the shape of a Washington fruit farmer — I am destined apparently always to share compartments with fruiterers — introduced himself, and dismissed the entire Soviet system as corrupt, and impractical, arguing that nothing is ever achieved in the world by political leaders or even by generals. 'Wars are won,' he insisted, 'by the poor bloody foot soldier, not by the commanders at staff headquarters.' Which was what was wrong with Russia — too much staff work, not enough getting down to it. At Khabarovsk he had been watching the inevitable workmen digging the customary hole in the ground, and computing the wastage of man hours involved. Abruptly, or perhaps because I wasn't following him blow by blow, he was in his own back orchard in the state of Washington, and dealing with the problem of casual labour at picking time.

'I employ,' he reminded me several times, 'the unemployed unemployable.' Each time he used the phrase, he closed his eyes as if with the effort of getting it spot on, and after each triumph he opened them again, like a cat basking by the fire. The unemployed unemployable where he came from consisted of three main streams — the alcoholic (from his point of view the best), the tobacco addict (more reliable, but likely to develop lung cancer on the site — he regaled me with gruesome anecdotes of the plight of several he had employed on their way to the morgue), and finally the last class, transients. But they, he affirmed, were really a pain in the arse. They had money in their pockets, and they wanted to choose the row they were to pick.

'That's no good to me. They're worse than Mexicans and niggers. Not, mind you, that I ever hire either. Nothing against them, just won't hire them, mind. Any more than I hire a man with money in his pocket, unless I'm pressed.'

I left him to go to the dining car, and when I returned, he had climbed into the upper bunk.

I sat on the edge of mine and communed with myself, perhaps as Lucifer had intended I should.

Russia knows none of this nonsense. No hate hangs in the air. It is a country where religion is practised, but not preached, as opposed to the West, where it is preached, but not practised. Does the Russian really love his neighbour as himself, I wondered. Is there no lunatic fringe, no muggings in the streets? Is there no hatred, envy or malice? One phrase Lucifer had used kept coming back to me. 'If I see a dead body, man, I just step over it.' So this, then, was America, this perhaps what London will become: the ghouls not dancing on the graves, but stepping over them carefully. This was Vietnam and Chicago, Grosvenor Square and Salisbury, Colin Jordan and Enoch Powell. This was Hell, and the vast, gentle, lobotomised land I was leaving — Heaven? In the upstairs bunk I heard a snore, or just possibly a chuckle. No, I told myself, it's not as simple as that.

In the morning we reached Nakhodka and sailed for Japan. In the bar that evening, the Devil was still holding forth about the iniquities of the system. One of our fellow passengers had been interrogated by the police for taking pictures of railway platforms. Before letting him embark they had confiscated all his films and nearly frightened the life out of him into the bargain.

'Cruel, that's what they are, cruel. All that long, difficult journey, and now nothing to show for it.'

'Stupid, ignorant, clumsy, how can they expect people to come to their wretched country when they behave like that?'

'All the same,' I told them, 'it does say in the regulations that you mustn't photograph railway stations.'

'What regulations?' they demanded. 'We never read any regulations. They make up the rules as they go along.'

'But doesn't everyone?'

The sea was a dead calm, the fishing boats put on their lights to lure the sardines. The moon rose over Japan. There was a party in the lounge, but no one went. They sat drinking at the bar, still arguing about their hosts, for although everything had to be paid for now in dollars, the ship was still Russian. A month is a long time. Most of the tourists were bored with Communism. Czechoslovakia still nagged their conscience. 'Supposing,' I asked them, 'there hadn't been a Lenin or a Stalin or a war, what sort of civilisation would have been possible?'

'Free enterprise, that's all they needed,' said the Devil. 'They would be in fine shape by now.'

'Like the rest of us?'

'What's wrong with the rest of us? Bloody sight better places than Russia.'

'You can say that again,' they echoed.

'The trouble with Russia is, it's a poor country. It will always be a poor country.'

102

I thought of the old ladies, sweeping up the leaves in the cold of Leningrad; of the grey crowds queuing for tea cups in Moscow. I thought of the dusty, unmade roads in Bukhara, and the smell of the café in Irkutsk, and then I thought of the children.

'Not as poor as all that,' I told them, 'not by a long chalk.'

Japan

I had no idea what I expected to find in Japan. Accepting with alacrity the offer of the American First National Bank of a lift from Yokohama to Tokyo, I climbed in between the young executive whom I had met on board, and his senior colleague who had come down to welcome him, and whom I naturally imagined would be prepared to point out the sights to us both. I have never put my trust in bank managers before, and was foolish to have done so on this occasion. Neither of them drew breath, nor looked out of the window at the strange landscape through which we passed. They talked shop.

'Wallace is now No. 2 in Beirut.'

'I'm glad. The rumour here was that he was going to be No. 3, but how does Lloyd feel about it?'

'Lloyd is hoping to go to Rome or Cairo or Timbuctoo, somewhere like that.'

'Some hope, with a wife like his.'

'I saw Lew in London. He just happened to be coming out of his office. There's a new structure chart. Did you get yours?'

'No.'

'The only reason I got mine was Richard kept pressing George at lunch. I gathered he didn't really want to show it to me.'

'How is George making out?'

'Hard to say. Some of his work is brilliant. He sees things differently from the rest of us, but, boy, some of his mistakes made my hair curl.'

'Tomorrow I'm having a photographer come in and take your picture.'

'Swell.'

'We'll have to airmail it rush to Seattle or we'll miss the deadline. Miss Pearce isn't too sold on holding the house chronicle, but I think

I've persuaded her. One has to play Miss Pearce along. First person I call on when I'm in Seattle. I took her back a kimono last year. She was tickled pink.'

'I'd like to see Miss Pearce in a kimono.'

'Just a plain one, nothing fancy.'

'I'd like to see anyone in a kimono,' I interrupted, plaintively.

'Tell me,' said the younger one, 'if you were going to route a major policy decision from here, would you go through Rome?'

'Bombay.'

'Bombay? Gee, that's a thought.'

I was thankful when we arrived at Tokyo. A beautiful hotel, standard-size bath towels, a seal over the toilet, television, room service, shoe cleaning facilities. In a daze of excitement I listened to the Forces Network, leafed through the excursion brochures, and decided to take a trip to Nikko.

Downstairs in the lobby next morning, I await the guide. At seven forty-five he hasn't arrived. In a panic I try to force my way into a limousine with two shining American ladies. I know there is a deadline for the train. I am bundled out. When my own bus arrives it is full. There is a scramble to get to the station. After that, it is just a question of following the flag. Our guide carries a small blue one. We follow it up the platform into the train, and at Nikko, out of the train into the bus. By now we have badges pinned on us — Sunrise Tours.

At the shrines the groups proliferate. Everyone is ticketed — Swiss Hoteliers, Honda Dealers, Tokyo Trips, U.S. Armed Forces Paymaster — Special Excursion. Japanese schoolchildren wear labels round their necks. The temple carvings are pretty — what one sees of them, which isn't much. There is a celebrated cat. When the sculptor had finished fashioning him they cut off his arms. Goodness, how we tourists enjoy torture. We are constantly taking off our shoes, and I am constantly wondering if I shall get mine back on in time. It takes me longer than most to tie shoelaces. I am back at school, the last child in the line, beset by anxiety, walking with the teacher. Shall I try walking with the guide? Where is he? Have I lost the blue flag? We are given minute cups of saki, but it is the temple dancing that really tests us. This dance is particularly popular, the guide informs us, but with whom he doesn't say. I have never seen such hideous women cavorting with such lack of interest.

We are fed in droves at the tourist hotel, then taken on a bus ride. Forty hairpin bends, three waterfalls and a joke from the guide about the brakes. Oh well, it's over at last.

105

Back in the hotel that evening I met Mr. Jones. If, like me, you are an actor, and sit around conspicuously − and how, alas, can I help doing that − in hotel foyers, sooner or later you can be sure of being accosted by strangers anxious to enquire your name for their own personal memory filing system. I told Mr. Jones my name, although he purported to be already familiar with it, and fell in gleefully with his suggestion that he should pay for dinner. One of the great things about being subjected to domestic currency regulations is that no one any longer expects an Englishman abroad to pay up − one isn't even expected to look pleasant. We adjourned to a smart bistro, Western style, and munched kobe steaks, a great local speciality. The cattle, so Mr. Jones informed me, are fed beer and subjected to a daily massage while still on the hoof. In England, of course, they continue to batter them with a rolling-pin long after they are dead. My kobe steak was delicious, and the meal was only slightly marred by Mr. Joe di Maggio coming over from the next table and enquiring courteously whether I was Francis L. Sullivan, an actor who has been dead for many years. I was able to reassure him, but my host realised the effort it had cost me.

'Tomorrow, perhaps,' he suggested, 'you would care to eat Japanese style.'

'I really can't,' I told him, 'impose on you for another meal, unless of course you insist. What time, and where?'

The next evening he picked me up once more in the Hilton lounge and transported me to Happo-En, where he had laid on a meal, Japanese-style. Accompanied by a Japanese lady about to marry his general manager, and the lucky fellow himself, we were ushered into a private dining-room, of rather meagre proportions, and furnished with low tables, rush matting and cushions. I had, of course, much against my will, already removed my shoes, remarking that in my country rush matting stands up to shoe leather. The great need when travelling in Japan is for elastic-sided boots and darning wool, to save face and toenails.

When I was much younger, and toured the English provinces, I was *accustomed* to living in bed-sitting-rooms. The front parlour and principal bedroom suite in the houses would be occupied by the vaudeville artistes. I was a straight man myself, and in those days was not so prone to resent not having the best of everything. After all, the vaudeville chaps paid more, and were entitled to superior accommodation. There was a sort of rough justice in the plan. But in the Happo-En I was certain that Mr. Jones was paying top prices, and couldn't help wondering whether there weren't better rooms, and

106

later on, whether there wasn't better food. The evening got off to a bad start when the Japanese lady who was to serve the meal appeared with a back rest for myself. I can sit up as straight as the next man. I was disappointed, too, at the age of the waitresses. I had expected young, nubile maidens, while our personal staff looked as if they had stepped from an amateur performance of *The Mikado*. Hefty, large ladies, they knelt beside me to prepare a disastrous indoor picnic.

There is nothing whatever to be said for a dish called suki-aki. Only once before have I ever essayed it, and that was with the great Molly Picon herself. We had been invited by the producer of a play called *Majority of One* which we were then rehearsing, to a genuine Japanese dinner. The ceremony took place in a house in Golders Green, a remote suburb of my capital. Half way through the banquet, when we had sampled the raw fish and other beastliness, Miss Picon was asked what she would like next. 'A doctor,' she told her host, and for me at any rate the evening was made. I didn't, naturally, need a doctor in Tokyo, nor had I the temerity to ask for one, but there was a moment of contretemps when Mr. Jones drew my attention to the fact that I was eating seaweed. Mistakenly believing that he was reprimanding me for a breach of etiquette, and that seaweed, like parsley, should be left on the plate, I spat it out, only to find my fellow guests continuing to masticate theirs with obvious enjoyment. Obviously my palate is at fault. It fails to appreciate tepid, stringy beef dipped in raw egg, or the extraordinary variety of dank vegetation which accompanies it on these occasions. I don't say the Japanese will eat anything, but they will have a damn good shot at it.

We finished the evening in a nightclub; the hostesses drank orange juice, persuaded us to buy them cuddly toys. It's a time-honoured routine, older than the temple dancing; the hard drink, the soft touch. It was very late when I got back to the hotel. Under my door I found a note.

'Dear Guest, We have been advised by the Tokyo Metropolitan Police that a student demonstration is slated to take place tomorrow within this area en route to the Diet Building. The time may be from 6 p.m. onward. The police department will provide adequate protection, but in the unlikely event that a few demonstrators filter through the police cordon, we would advise guests not to antagonize them, take photographs, or in any case leave the hotel premises while the demonstration is in progress. The Management.'

When 6 p.m. came I decided to reconnoitre. There was no sign of any excitement. In the foyer I met Mr. Bagshot, an American professor at the University, who had been rehearsing his students in *The Glass Menagerie* since April, and now found them rather wooden. A patient, gentle fellow who had some years before gone native, but now once again lived Western-style. His companion asked me whether I would like to go and look at the riots.

'Not much,' I told him, 'not at all, in fact. What's their purpose?'

'They are demonstrating against Nixon.'

'Nothing of the kind,' said Mr. Bagshot, 'they are demonstrating against the Government who are still holding their fellow students from the last three demonstrations.'

They took me to the Shinkyuku district for dinner. I have never seen so many pin tables. The Japanese play with ball bearings. There was at one time a surplus of ball bearings, and local ingenuity put them to good use. Baskets and baskets full of ball bearings fed into the machines, recovered, counted and exchanged for cigarettes – an economy of its own. We ate mushrooms obtainable only at this time of the year, and in small quantities, alas. Afterwards we visited the 'gay' bars. The Japanese tolerate homosexuality, live with it, and judging from the noise and laughter, learn to love it.

But of all the people I met in Tokyo, none explained Japan better to me than a fellow countryman called Seyman. It was he who drove me to Hakone, who insisted we took the river steamer across the lake and the cable car up the mountains, who showed me Fujiama. 'To see the sacred mountain on a clear day,' he told me, 'is a very great privilege.' Nothing becomes Japan better than Fujiama. I was prepared to dislike the Japanese. I am nervous of a people who laugh so frequently. I hadn't realised that in their own country they have so much to laugh at. Here their gaiety is infectious. The British are preoccupied, the Russians serene, the Japanese are gay. Sunday in the Ginza in Tokyo was quite unlike Sunday anywhere else in the world. The enormous department stores, decorated with tropical fish tanks and enormous chrysanthemums, their roof gardens taken over by the children, their floors and restaurants and art galleries, the elegance of the display counters. I leapt on and off the escalators, priced the kimonos, fingered the jade, coveted the cameras and bought the toys.

'What is the secret?' I asked Mr. Seyman. 'What makes Japan tick? Is it a bomb?'

'I don't think so,' he told me. 'I don't think it will all blow up. There is very little discontent. You see, they never get rid of anyone, and they are careful to see that no one loses face. If you run a business here, you must leave staff relations in their hands. The

Americans and ourselves simply don't understand the system. Each year, when they take on their employees in the spring, they take on an obligation to them. It's something the Western capitalist system has failed to do. Here they consider us bad employers of labour. We drive people and when they break down, we sack them. Here the emphasis is in keeping everyone and everything in running order.'

I could have stayed a long time in Tokyo, but it was time to be thinking of getting home. On the way I stopped off at Hong Kong. From my hotel bedroom I looked out on a cricket ground. Here, where there is barely room for a postage stamp, children in shorts were running round in a circle while a great British games master hurled rugby footballs at them. 'Catch it, you clowns,' he yelled. 'Come along, fellows, don't slack.'

The *Hong Kong Times* is full of the announcements of the Royal Hong Kong Jockey Club's forthcoming meeting, and outlining the complicated instructions for those wishing to be admitted to the Enclosures. The blackest type of all reserves the right of admission. The Enclosure within the Enclosure is what the British are always seeking for themselves. For the Americans on leave from Vietnam they offer the Chinese. Electric signs advertising the honky tonks proliferate. Parts of the city seem to be nothing but an enormous brothel. The streets are full of stalls marketing shoddy goods; the children never go to bed as long as there is still a customer. With a fourteen-hour day, without unions, without compulsory education, everybody manages to get by somehow.

I spent the afternoon with the Hong Kong Water Police. They wear shorts and search the dhows and junks with the keenness of Boy Scouts. Only the Communist boats from Macao pass unchallenged. 'We don't want to tangle with them,' they tell you. What they are looking for usually is dynamite. The Chinese have a habit of throwing it into the water to stun the fish, and another habit of taking it home with them in the evenings. There's a good deal of dynamite in Hong Kong just at present. At dinner parties, the discussion is always about China. 'If you want to know what is really going on there,' they tell me, 'have a look at Macao.'

I went there in a hydrofoil. Formalities were minimal. I wandered round and marvelled at the squalor, and that there could be so many crabs. It was the season for crabs. Everywhere men, women and children were tying them up with raffia and popping them into wicker baskets. In some stores they held them up in front of an electric bulb, but I never discovered why. I drifted into the Casino, which is moored beside the junks, and became absorbed in roulette. I only just managed to catch the hydrofoil back to Hong Kong. Although I had glimpsed China across the water, I had discovered absolutely nothing about it. I was no longer curious. It was time to go home.

One day I shall publish the definitive guide on what not to see or do abroad. Avoid, for preference, any place connected with a legend. 'Here the simple fishermen threw themselves off the cliff.' They may have done, but it will involve a steep climb for the rest of us. Avoid towers for the same reason, and son et lumière, and plays acted in a foreign language and buildings entirely rebuilt since the war. Beware of government-sponsored stores and light operas. Limit yourself to one cathedral, one picture gallery and one giant Buddha a week. Remember, a tourist accepts, a traveller selects.

Las Vegas

Fifty years ago, give or take a few, after an appalling luncheon of cold ham and stodge, my housemaster at Wellington College summoned me to his study and sent me packing. 'You're not looking well, boy. You need a holiday,' he told me, and a few hours later I stood beside my tuck-box on an empty platform, praying that the train would arrive before I woke up. It was the best holiday I ever had, and in some ways it was to last forever. At least, I never went back to school.

I am a great believer in the idea that lightning can, and often does, strike twice in the same place, but alas, no one has ever again sped me on my way in such a totally unexpected fashion. One day, perhaps, I shall walk through the stage door of a theatre in which I am performing to find the proprietor waiting for me with an airline ticket. It doesn't have to be the proprietor, the stage door-keeper will do just as well. I would take my dismissal from anyone and start my holiday as a holiday should be started, on the spur of the moment. A holiday which is planned in advance isn't really a holiday at all, just another engagement. All those elaborate arrangements finalised in January for a brief fortnight at Frinton in August with one's loved ones, are self-defeating. By all means take the children for a paddle, but remember that for most of us it is part of our working year, and very often the part where we work hardest.

The ideal holiday should start as my first — and I begin to think only real — holiday started, just before the exams, or halfway through a conversation with one's bank manager, or getting the tea ready for the kids. That is the moment to put down the phone or the tray and get out fast. A holiday should be a walk-out, a wildcat strike. Leave the pieces, you can pick them up later. Get away. But where? Norway? I suppose there are people who enjoy those roofless grottoes and the midnight sun which never seems to get up high enough to warm them, but for me there is a limit to the simple life, and that limit is often exceeded around the Arctic Circle. The scenery is magnificent and when I was making a picture there, I was never allowed to forget it. There was always someone at my elbow reminding me how much they were enjoying the vista, and expecting me to do the same. Beauty is in the eye of the beholder, but what makes the beholders themselves so unattractive? Nature lovers out on a hike dress worse than coursing enthusiasts at Altcar.

But back to the stage door and the airline ticket. Where would I fly to? Now, this minute, tomorrow or the day after? The answer is always the same — Las Vegas. The man who doesn't gamble has not been born. Life is contrived in such a way that to gamble is as necessary for survival as to breathe. People who profess to despise the more overt forms of gambling, like roulette and marriage, might find Vegas was not the place for them. It is, however, *the* place for me. When I first went there in the thirties it consisted of a couple of saloons at a crossroads leading to the silver mines, and for the first time I watched silver dollars being thrown around by men who kept their safety helmets on at the bar. It was a hideous little town. It was also attractive. Today it is still the ugliest, most attractive resort in the world.

On a fine Labour Day, and it is nearly always fine in Vegas, you can see a quarter of a million tourists on the Strip, or at least in the hotels that are built along it. Uniformly hideous, improbably named, and almost indistinguishable from each other, they are spaced at a nicely-judged distance so that to travel between them except by taxi-cab is uncomfortable in the heat and the occasional sandstorm. There is nothing to choose between the Stardust and the Thunderbird, the Dunes and Caesars Palace. They are all extremely comfortable, expertly staffed around the clock, scrupulously clean and air-conditioned. Each has a pool compulsorily vacated by the guests at seven o'clock, a restaurant in which one can hear Frank Sinatra or Dean Martin or our own Tom Jones, and a casino which never closes and in which the crap tables, the pontoon dealers and the roulette wheels are all assembled in a mathematical ratio. There are just so many of each, spaced just so far apart and presumably patronised by just so many customers at any hour of the day or night. Somewhere there is an architect who works out the arrangements, and since all the casinos are identically arranged, must be the sole arbiter on such niceties.

As in all deserts, great importance is attached to drink, and most men and some women carry a glass in their hand when moving

How The Other Half Loves, with Brian Miller and Jan Holden (*Angus McBean*)

With Eric Morecambe and Ernie Wise (*BBC Copyright*)

Dame Gladys Cooper

Dame Gladys with her daughter Jo
now Mrs. Robert Morley

The young
Robert Morley

With grandson Hugo (*Alan Clifton for Playboy magazine*)

The gourmet (*Punch*)

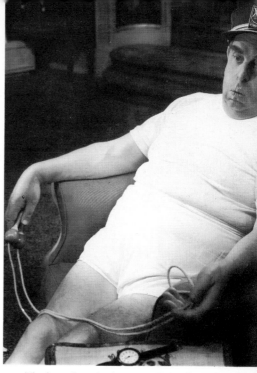

The keep-fit enthusiast (*Punch*)

A musing Morley (*Reading Evening Post*)

In Red Square, Moscow

Bukhara: 'Russia was full of water melons . . .'

With Rudolf Nureyev in a Toronto restaurant (*Toronto Star Syndicate*)

around the hotel or walking to their cars. They are not encouraged to take them with them into the swimming pools, but often do so. Carrying a glass in his hand reminds an American that he is on holiday and to be with Americans on holiday is why I go to Vegas. For I, too, like to be reminded of the hell on earth in which most of us survive. And we do survive, often despite excruciating difficulties, in acute despair and unbelievable squalor. We survive the wars and the peace. We survive childhood and middle age and we very nearly survive death. We survive love and hate, inflicting appalling cruelties on ourselves and each other. We are gloomy, sullen, silent and lachrymose, and in Vegas we are often gay, noisy and drunk. We are as brave as lions. We shiver in our shoes, but we also occasionally dance in them. We are raucous and boorish and we are alive because we don't know what else to be, and I like to be reminded of all this. I don't want to be reminded of trees and mountains and pink-footed geese. I want to be reminded of what I am — a hopeless, horrible human being. That's why every now and then I want to go back to Vegas and have a look at myself.

New York

Back in New York after an absence of three years, I found the city much as I remembered it. Outside St. Patrick's Cathedral a woman staggered under a jumbo crucifix, campaigning against the Pope, and watched by a mounted policeman and a few incurious spectators. The rest of us admired a huge vacuum cleaner, coping with a solitary cigarette stub which defied all efforts to remove it, until the operator finally bent down and lifted it from the sidewalk, whereupon we clapped happily and marched on.

When I first glimpsed New York from the traditional viewpoint of the Hudson River all those years ago, it seemed brand new, a towering city, built now for tomorrow, but time has caught up faster than expected, at least by me. New York is old and shabby and painted like a tart, the paint sprayed on by her children in spraygun profusion, on the buses, on the memorials, on the skyscrapers, the post boxes, the litter bins, even the trees in Central Park, anywhere in fact which can sustain the message that Paul had Susan last night, that Christ is coming, that Fat Samson has been. Very little is decipherable; either the children never learnt to write or the spraygun is more difficult to operate than a pen. The city fathers are reported to be outraged by such vandalism, but there is little they can do to preserve the concrete from this sudden drive towards personalization. Indeed, solid citizens such as myself feel at times an almost irresistible urge to participate. Passing a stationary and unattended police car, I was seized by an overwhelming desire to improve the body work with a cipher of my initials, but fortunately perhaps for me I was without the equipment.

Instead I wandered into Rumplemayers to devour a chocolate ice cream soda and remember the moment of panic when, sitting in the same corner thirty-five years earlier I had almost, but not quite decided to quit before the first night of Oscar Wilde. Then I had left my soda untasted, staggered to my feet and somehow got myself to the Fulton Theatre, but now I sucked happily on the straws, gazing round at the unchanged scene. The same outsized stuffed cuddlies were displayed on the shelves and here, lest there should be confusion, I must make it clear that I am referring to the real toys, not the habituées of the cake shop, who still descend from their eyries on the fiftieth floor of the St. Moritz and pass through the lobby each afternoon to sample the Danish pastry and the éclairs.

There are still things you mustn't do in New York, like trying to be funny. If there are jokes to be made, your host will see to it. The exceptions, of course, are on the chat shows; here the visitor is expected, nay commanded, to make the running, to give his opinion, to repeat his anecdotes, to express pleasure and confusion with the local customs. Go on, hit us, the hosts invite, tell us why things are so much better in England, and we strive to obey. For ninety minutes, and with endless interruption from our sponsors, I discuss with Cavett every topic under the sun, from Hetty King's childhood to dreaming about the Monarch. Once, years ago, on just such a forum I opined that Australia was larger than the U.S., and Cavett pretends the remark still rankles. It was an honest opinion at the time, unlike most I parade on these occasions. Most of the time one spins a web of improbability, flattering and scolding the American way of life, and knowing absolutely nothing of it.

Afterwards, when the programme is safely on tape, I go out to dinner with the Wallachs, whose way of life has altered very little all the years I have known them. They live on Riverside Drive, a family enjoying New York, the children growing up, putting down roots in the asphalt jungle and flourishing. They study Spanish and French and pure mathematics, guitar playing, tap dancing, film making and advanced geology. They have majored in American Constitution and after the turkey and the strawberry shortcake, they withdraw to their bedrooms to continue the homework and telephone their friends about the problems of Cuba or good old Wystan. They are clever children, this is a clever city, and they are making the most of it, and one day they will be able to tell their grandchildren about the days when their country was on the verge of despair and won through.

Toronto

At two o'clock in the morning, if you open your
window and listen,
You will hear the feet of the Wind that is going to
call the sun.
And the trees in the shadow rustle and the trees in
the moonlight glisten,
And though it is deep, dark night, you feel that the
night is done.

I suppose it is possible I might have followed Kipling's instructions if I hadn't, as is usually the case when I wake at two in the morning with indigestion, been filled with unreasoning panic. This, I told myself, is it, curtains. You have overeaten once too often, you won't even see the sun.

The night before, we had buried *How The Other Half Loves* in Toronto, and after the final drink and the admonishments to the others, who mostly seemed to be taking the bus trip across America and out the other side, Peter Bridge and I left with the takings to have a square meal at about two in the morning, a habit to which we have both become addicted in a city where they eat late and heavily.

In the restaurant, the proprietor himself was cooking, always a sign that the food is going to be on the rich side, and Nureyev occupied the adjacent table. We guardedly compared grosses and were both elated, not so much that we were leaving Canada, a country of which in a month I had become fond, but that we were leaving with the money. To go into a city and having held it to ransom, to have taken the money and run, is part for me at least of the deep satisfaction of my trade. I remember the pride with which I fingered the first free rail ticket they ever gave me, forty-five years ago, and I still think it wonderful that I can make people pay to see me act.

116

We are all gipsies, and there is no more dedicated gipsy than Nureyev, and no one who travels further across the stage and the world; next week he told me he was dancing in Melbourne. He had allowed himself five days to get there and rehearse. I asked him whether he couldn't break his journey. 'For three hours,' he told me 'in Hawaii.' I asked him what else there was for him but dancing, and he seemed puzzled. I told him I was going back to London via Vegas, not a direct route, but that I enjoyed the scenery on the way, and he smiled politely. I suppose we both thought the other rather mad, and when I enquired finally if he ever talked about dancing to the students of the local Universities, as I sometimes talked about acting, he said, 'Not yet. When I am old and don't know whether I am still standing or sitting down, then I might.'

I can't pretend I ever wanted to be a dancer, but lying awake at two in the morning when all was not well, I thought back and wished perhaps I had had more dedication, more purpose, more self-denial. A man with indigestion craves a confessor. I like to think I take my calling seriously, but I know I don't. There are some things that matter, dressing-rooms for instance. When we'd arrived in the town, I inspected the dressing-rooms at the Royal Alexandra, a nice old theatre taken over recently and run by a local character called Honest Ed Mirvish. I wish perhaps that London management had as much drive as Comrade Mirvish, and then perhaps I don't. His principal business and interest is a huge cut-price supermarket of quite startling drabness. Everything very close together so that the customers keep knocking down the piles of saucers and cooking pans so that they can be picked up and still further reduced. Every morning there is a breakfast special, a mystery giveaway, and housewives queue up excitedly for Honest Ed's bargain. It may be cornflakes or pianos on the menu, but whatever it is they buy it in this enormously aggressive sales territory. On the other hand, Ed gives nothing away in the theatre, not even complimentary seats. He maintains he is not a theatre man and has never heard of the custom. Around the corners he owns a number of restaurants, of which the most famous is Ed's Warehouse, which was just that, until Ed moved in, bought fifty tons of steaks a week, had them weighed carefully and cooked carefully and served them to the customers. Losses in the theatre are made up on the Prime New York Tenderloin cuts, and I must say in all fairness, they are delicious.

However, in the theatre when I arrived there wasn't such a thing as an easy chair. I am fairly well acquainted with such rigorous training, but never accede to it. 'When the dressing-rooms are furnished and

117

carpeted,' I told them, 'we'll start with the lighting rehearsal.' There was a brief pause, not as might happen in England for consternation, but for Ed to muster his army. Then, hey presto, the furniture van arrived. We did fantastic business in Toronto, even for Ed, but that man keeps his head. I had hardly sat down after the performance on the last night and poured myself a drink, when there was a knock on the door and the furniture men were back, asking if I'd finished with the chair. 'But,' I told them, 'Michael Redgrave, *Sir* Michael Redgrave is here on Monday. He's already arrived, more important he's seen the drapes and the carpet. What's he going to say when he finds the place stripped?' The brokers men were firm. Michael would have to fight his own battle.

On the opening night Ed had given the company a party after the show, in the Chinese portion of his warehouse. It wasn't the high-spirited affair we had hoped for, attended by the café society of Toronto and the Governor General. There wasn't even the British Trade Commissioner, a matter which caused me to speak fairly sharply to him when we did meet on the last Friday of our visit.

'How do you think you've helped,' I charged, 'aren't you supposed to promote the British?' but he pleaded ignorance, as is usual in diplomatic circles, for which so he informed me, he qualifies.

'Never knew you were coming,' he told me blithely, 'I often give a party when I know the theatricals are on, but I've been in Montreal.' Montreal is all of forty minutes away and we pretend, or rather assert, that British Theatre is one of our main tourist traps, but not to worry, at least he is more highly regarded than some previous holders of the office. The wife of an early incumbent terrified the local British tradesmen by always producing her visiting card and demanding a discount on anything purchased by her.

At Ed's party, where I'd hinted to the company that we were going to meet the residents, there was only Ed himself and his wife and a press agent and a lady whose identity I never discovered, but who assured me that she travelled south like the birds when the weather turned cold.

'We go to Florida, we have a house there.'

'Miami?' I asked mischievously — there's a difference, particularly if you live in Palm Beach.

'Not Miami,' she corrected me with a slight shudder, 'I have never seen Miami. Some people motor that way, but we always send the car on ahead with the chauffeur, and fly.'

'It would mean him leaving two or three days before you, then?' I asked, determined to get as far in as I dared.

'A week,' she told me, 'it's a beautiful car and we don't like it being driven all out.'

'Tell me,' I said, 'when you arrive at the airfield, is the car there to meet you?'

'Oh yes,' she said, 'the car is there by that time.'

'What an ingenious idea,' I congratulated her effusively, 'I must try it myself one day,' and left her preening herself in the gloom. All restaurants in Toronto are pitch black, and Ed's are no exception. Food, like money perhaps, is better made and consumed in the dark.

Later on, after the first night was over, we met people and went out to parties, although it is difficult to discover the exact stratum of Toronto society we explored. Our hosts tended to ask more or less the same crowd and to serve lasagne. They were immensely kind and lived, one gathered, pleasant, detached lives in pleasant, detached houses. To find out what life is really like in Canada, one had as usual abroad, to rely on the taxi drivers, a race to which I am particularly well-disposed. Nowadays as soon as you walk down the endless corridors at the airport you are what is technically called 'on' in our business — expected to give your views on a city and civilisation you have only glimpsed from the air and the cab driving you to the television centre. You only talk to the talk jockey and the cabby. Luckily in Toronto the latter seldom let you down.

Actors arriving in Toronto usually flatter the Civic and the O'Keefe Centres, especially if they are playing the O'Keefe, which I wasn't, so thought I'd give it a miss. It is in point of fact a manager's dream and an actor's nightmare, thousands of seats comfortably spaced and the distance from the stage except for the first ten rows, total. A twitch of the eyebrows there — and I am forever twitching mine — would mean exactly nothing. The Civic Centre is quite a job. I got myself conducted round by the head guide, a lovely girl who earns a fortune and is in love with a computer in the basement. Most Canadian women are in love with computers; they sit talking to them all day and watching for the answer coming up like a body surfacing out of treacle in one of those witch balls they give children to wish and ask a question and turn upside down to read if the wish will come true.

The computer in the Civic Centre was asked fun questions in my honour, but I didn't think it was impressed by my visit. Its answers were terse and schoolmastery and the work never seemed done. It kept admonishing 'Information not available', or 'Rephrase' or 'Select'. There is a fortune waiting for the man who introduces the polite, the obsequious computer for the top executive and who, like the butler in Lonsdale's celebrated play, calls everyone Milord and is never contradicted.

The Civic Centre was built as a picture postcard illustration, an enormously successful and light-hearted pageant consisting of elliptical towers resembling, once it is pointed out to you, the human eye, very tall, very slim, very chic and immensely impractical. It was designed in open competition by a Finn who would surely have laughed all the way to the bank, if he hadn't been overtaken by wolves — in his case, alas, a heart attack — and died just about three weeks before the opening ceremony. In front of it is a very much patronised ice rink for the natives to bone up on their ice hockey, and at thirty-five million dollars, or whatever the building cost, they will be some time, even in Canada, getting their money's worth, but it is gay, it is beautiful and I wish London had anything half so extravagant. But I suppose the L.C.C. officials would jib at having to travel down fifty-seven floors, even in an express elevator, in order to cross a gracious patio and travel up thirty-nine more to have a chat and a cup of char with an opposite number.

This is a city of skycrapers, tall black towers standing back to back on tiptoe, cheating about which is the taller. It is a lonely city, a drugstore city, where the cheap counter food is munched by sad, lonely women already preparing at six in the evening for bed and television. The television is terrible, worse, if that is possible, than in the United States, a constant stream of advertisements for laxatives. The uptight city of all uptight cities, I told myself, before I knew it a little better. A country is judged on its television, it is the first thing the visitor switches on when he gets to his room, as he used to try the taps and flush the lavatory. Nowadays he leaves the television running, and it is still running when he walks out a month later, a stream of pitiless banality never allowing the sucker a break, let alone an even one.

The high spots of Canadian television are not the chat shows or the old films or the endless quizzes, but the weather reports. These are by far the most dramatic, the most expert. At the beginning, the weather men themselves appear to be outside, actually sampling the climate; halfway though the programmes, they move into the studios and draw isobars with both hands on a plate glass screen and write their messages mirror style, so that we can understand that tomorrow in Buffalo the high will be around the twenties and there will be snow flurries, strong winds along the lake, a few sunny spells and a forty-five per cent chance of precipitation, other than the snow, naturally. Most important of all is the temperature given right through the day and night on the hour. It is a temptation for the visitor who may search in vain for the action to believe that in this land of theirs, vast cataclysms overwhelm the Canadian geese and a man who is not sufficiently briefed with the weather forecast may boil or suddenly freeze to death in downtown Hamilton, but this I understand very rarely happens. No, the explanation is more prosaic, the weather service is complimentary, along with the second cup of coffee, and the television station takes a brief halt from customer bashing to try and persuade itself that it cares.

One word about the weather, which while I was in Toronto seemed much the same as anywhere else in the world, changeable, and we have done. High above the city and in full view of all stands a pylon with a lighted dome. This dome changes colour like a chameleon: red means rain, white snow, amber caution. Lights travelling upwards denote rising temperature, in the opposite direction that it is getting chilly. On a perfect day, a really perfect day, the whole thing switches itself off. Satisfied one morning that all was well, or that the beacon hadn't just broken down, which later, alas, proved to be the case, I decided to take the Wonderful Autumn Mystery Trip provided by Greyhound Buses, and view the maple leaves in their technicolour magnificence. Used as I am to an autumn of fading brown, I found the display rather over-theatrical. Eventually I suppose the leaves fall off like other leaves and have to be swept up, but meanwhile the other passengers travelled with tissue paper and would return from the comfort station or drive-ins with fronds of scarlet which they proceeded to insert between the leaves of scrap-books they happened to have with them.

Canadians, like Russians, dream of possessing a dacha and presumably a maple of their own one day. The lakesides are already littered with small bungalows of those new-type pioneers who seek at weekends to flee environmental pollution and make the two-hour journey from Toronto to Lake Muskoka holding their breath and defying exhaust fumes as they proceed bumper to bumper: the lemmings of our modern society on the way to the water's edge. Some of the houses around the lake are rather more than bungalows, and as we glimpsed them reverently from the pleasure steamer included in the price of the fare, our guide named the lucky owners along Millionaires' Row with the obsequiousness which was once afforded to the homes of the stars in Beverly Hills. He emphasised that these were summer palaces only. In the winter the lake freezes and the ski doers roar across the ice, pollution returns, but the millionaires are fled to Florida. 'This mansion,' he told us, 'is in the occupancy of Doctor

121

Bones, the celebrated Ontario Orthopaedic Surgeon and founder of the Doctor Bones Clinic in that city.' Those of us who believe that medicine and the law are what TV once appeared to be to Lord Thomson, smile at each other cynically when informed that the next mansion has seven bedrooms, three open fireplaces, a sitting-room twenty by forty feet, and is owned by a lawyer from Pittsburg. We strain our eyes to make out remote figures on the private jetty, wondering whether all is well with the children of such manifestly wealthy parents.

Canadian children, whether fishing off their private piers or selling newspapers downtown in Yonge Street, lending a disquietingly Dickensian image to the city, look pretty fit, are pretty fit, I imagine. Better than our lot, I tell myself, liable to go further, more fairly educated, I imagine, certainly stronger. These are outdoor children, skiing children, hunting children, hockey children, football children, swimming children, who'll make mincemeat of our kids if they ever meet them, just look at the size they come in.

But in some curious way they are corrupted by the great outdoors and grow up to pull the venetian blinds, lock the windows, turn on the air conditioning and move around only in motors. Perhaps it is because the Canadians don't keep dogs and so are never taken out for walks.

Niagara, when I finally got around to it, and I had purposely been saving it up as the highlight of my visit, Niagara is pure Walt. It is impossible to believe that the little man didn't have a hand in it. All around you are the towers and the waxworks, the adventure rides across the whirlpool and to the bottom of the falls and best of all, you put on black mackintoshes and wellington boots and waterproof bonnets over paper caps and you are away down the shaft to the tunnel right under the torrent. You stand in the dank, dark tube and imagine it collapsing, with you the one it falls upon, and you listen to the roar and feel the spray and peer through the mist, and if you are me, tell a party of ladies dressed like yourself as if for a Black Mass, that it's due to be turned off in another ten minutes, and then scurry on ahead to pack into the elevator which brings you back to the souvenir shop. They did turn it off once apparently, to inspect the erosion and clean the rocks; it must have been an awful let-down to have been there that morning, but for us all was well, the horse-shoe falls were in full spate. This is real Lillian Gish country, we told each other. They talk a good deal of the lives the dragon has claimed — about eight sacrifice themselves willingly each year, climbing the low railing, crossing a few feet of turf and they're in. The bodies

122

come up three days later, a few miles down stream, you can set your clock by them apparently, that is, once you know the hour they submerged. They tell about the little boy in the lifejacket who bounced over and managed to survive, the only one who did. They talk of Blondin and all the times he crossed on his tightrope and what fun he had pretending to slip and stopping for champagne, and how once when he carried his manager on his back, he under-estimated the fellow's weight and nearly tipped him into the drink. Actors like that story; we all carry a manager on our back.

There is a night club in Toronto that advertises it possesses the only naked chef in the world. Actually, the night we went they had changed the slogan to the only naked hat-check girl in the world, so I was a bit disappointed when we were received by an elderly lady in discreet evening gown.

'Surely you should be undressed,' I told her.

She smiled patiently and explained she was the mother-in-law of the proprietor and not a party to such frivolity. 'My son-in-law is a good boy, but tonight he's gone to the pictures. That's why we've changed the poster.' We enjoyed ourselves as best we could, despite the absence of the advertised attraction and apparently a liquor licence, and I was asked on stage, introduced to the other five patrons and invited to paint one of the models with a spraygun. Deprived for once of inspiration, I executed a formal pattern of noughts and crosses on her torso and acknowledged the applause. On the way out, mother-in-law, suddenly smitten by conscience, inquired if we really wanted to see a naked hat-check girl, but we told her we were content.

I don't know whether all Toronto ladies are on such obviously good terms with their sons-in-law, but Canadians are a great race for quarrelling with their fathers. The taxi driver taking me to the theatre one evening turned himself on along with the clock and gave a vivid blow-by-blow account of his early life with a father who loved to use his dukes, and cried whenever Queen Victoria's name was mentioned.

'Why did he do that?' I asked.

'Because my old man was an actor, same as you — a rough man, really rough, everyone ran away, first my mother when I was five, and then all my brothers and sisters as soon as they grew up. Finally I joined the army just to get away, and even then I was afraid he might come after me, so I told the adjutant that my old man was senile, and for the first time I felt safe. He died right along the street. I was holding his hand. He didn't seem to know me, I guess that's why he was quiet. "I could do with a shot," he kept saying. I had a hip flask and the nurse finally let me give him a swig from it, and he choked and died. The nurse kept patting me on the back and telling me it was all right. She thought I was crying, see, but I was laughing. Just about the best thing that ever happened to me.'

Then there was the actor at a party, telling me how he walked out in the traditional Canadian manner.

'Goodbye, Father, next time I see you, you'll be in your coffin.'

'Better make sure, son, better make sure or I'll kill you, that's for certain.'

'You must,' I told him, 'have been a real fun family.' O'Neill never wrote more meaningful dialogue.

We couldn't have found a happier resting place than Toronto for *How The Other Half Loves*. After nearly a thousand performances, the little piece was still going great guns, and actors like nothing better than being stopped in the street and asked how to get tickets. I don't suppose we found out much about Canada or the Canadians, but we learnt a little about a country of which the English know nothing, which is not surprising when you think how little Canadians seem to know about their land either. They insist that Toronto is unique, a booming economy, and tend to shrug off the alarming unemployment figures. 'Not here,' they tell you, 'the only unemployed here are the bums and the dropouts, there's work waiting for everyone.'

But some of the vacancies advertised are unattractive; to work for instance in a team of fish scourers, knee deep in brine, at thirty-five cents an hour, or with four other women, packing turkeys. One cleaves the bird, a second puts her hand in and rips out the entrails, a third hoses the carcase.

'And the fourth,' I asked, 'what does the fourth do?'

'Cuts off the head, I guess.' The ladies work round the clock, twenty-five seconds a bird, eight hours a day.

In some ways it's still a rough country. When the settlers arrived here from Pennsylvania, the forests were so thick they couldn't see the sun and no birds sang, but the Indians were all around them. They cut down the trees and settled the Indians, they built log cabins and went on to build roads and houses and eventually the most famous civic centre in the world. In fifty years they had steamboats on the lake and a city to be proud of, and they are still proud of it. These great, cheerful, enormous men and their diminutive wives may not be as elegant as the French or hustle as much as the Americans, they may not, as Prince Philip once unwisely told them to, have quite made up their minds about us, but they still drink the Queen's health in water and even if they are happiest with a label pinned to their lapel, explaining who they are and what convention they are attending, they are our friends, our allies, and in some ways our creation. We owe them and the late General Wolfe a good deal.

The Fairy Penguins of Phillip Island

We tourists are given to sudden enthusiasms, and just as well for the tour organisers that such is the case. We are content, nay eager, to sit in a bus for two or three hours and be trundled to, for instance, the Eureka Stockade. None of us has ever heard of Eureka, few can visualise a stockade, and are only mildly disappointed to arrive in Ballarat and discover that today it is a small green park containing a massive obelisk inscribed with the names of the fallen.

For a few days afterwards we are aware that here the gold miners and the army and possibly the police came to fisticuffs and worse in the middle of the last century, and that a half-hearted protest by the citizenry was whole-heartedly put down by the executive.

It happened all over the world; it still happens. No doubt before long a park will be laid out in Derry and a stone cross erected to mark Bloody Sunday. 'What was that, then?' the tourists will ask, and if they are on a conducted tour, they will be told.

I am a man who keeps close to the guide: I like to hear every word. I feel I am getting my money's worth. I don't remember what has been said, naturally, but I like to pretend that I am an instant historian or an instant zoologist, which brings me to the Fairy Penguins.

I have always had a horror of fairies, not human fairies, but the dreadful little creatures who dance at the bottom of the garden. I cannot abide fairy stories, I loathe Peter Pan, I am nauseated by pictures of the little people cobwebbing about on the grass.

Penguins do not fill me with the same feelings of abhorrence as fairies, but I am not fond of them either, or let us say I quickly tire of watching them. 'Next slide, please,' I tell Peter Scott. Penguins are so easy to photograph that naturalists always bring back more feet of them on film than any of us can reasonably digest.

Leaving Melbourne one morning on our pilgrimage to Phillip

126

Island, the shrine of fairy penguins, I was instantly in sympathy with the Japanese party who had preceded us the week before and in the same motor had infuriated our chauffeur by demanding to be driven home as soon as the first fairy penguin had emerged from the surf and made his way unsteadily up the beach. I defended their attitude and agreed with their verdict, delivered on the trip home. 'Once you have seen one fairy penguin, you have seen them all.' Not that we were expecting to see them all; at this time of the year a lot of them have departed with their chicks. I can no longer remember where they are headed for, possibly just the sea itself until summer returns, or just possibly spring, and then they are back to Phillip Island to burrow and breed.

To enjoy our excursion to the full and because we wanted to spend as long as possible in anticipation of the inevitable anti-climax induced by the spectacle of a cloud of penguins walking across the sand, we took the long way round to the Island.

We caught a ferry at a place called rather aptly, Stoney Point. The jetty was deserted when we arrived, save for a tramp steamer loading caravans. Like most jetties in Australia, it had fallen into disrepair and had to be negotiated with extreme caution. The coast of this land is littered with man's aspirations to reach the water on dry feet and always a fatal collapse of a pier or the splintering of boards has doomed the enterprise. Nothing is ever repaired; once it has collapsed it is, in the vernacular, 'given away'. When the ferry arrived we were the sole passengers. The Captain, unreasonably buoyant considering the weather, insisted that I steered and seemed hugely delighted by my efforts to collide with a tanker.

Cowes, when we reached it, turned out to be a small seaside town entirely dependent on the birds. A festival of penguins is not easy to sustain, the birds after all only appear briefly for about twenty minutes and the rest of the day must be spent viewing seals through a telescope or buying postcards and tea cloths. For us the time was brief, the penguins were due in ten minutes. We drove to the beach in an agony of fear that the creatures might have decided on an early night and we should be too late. We need not have worried. Right on the button they appeared in the rays of the searchlight sweeping the waves. They paused at the water's edge for what seemed an eternity, coyly retreated and then advanced again. Penguins can be quite a tease. The night was bitterly cold. I became convinced that I was about to catch pneumonia, but after coming all this way, I dared not retreat until the ceremony was over. I stayed while the penguins stumbled and rolled over and were assisted to their feet by kindly

127

penguin concessionaires. I listened to the interminable commentary. I watched the confusion of a small child caught in the searchlight who didn't understand they were begging him to leave the enclosure reserved for the birds and allow them to proceed. When he finally grasped the enormity of his crime, he ran screaming into the darkness towards his mother or possibly the waves. At last it was over, the last smelly little bird safely holed up in the sand, save for the few stragglers who would be run over by the cars leaving the scene. I got back into mine, shivering, apprehensive and determined never again if I could possibly help it to look at a penguin, fairy or even king-size.

The Inquisition is Alive and Well . . .

There is, in the middle of the Basque country, a mountain plain called Urbasa, much favoured by film companies when engaged on costume drama. It is a convenient locale to deploy the talents of middle-aged British actors, along with a few thousand Spanish horsemen. Alas, the plain, though admirably devoid of electricity pylons and television aerials, is not particularly favoured by the weather.

On location for *Cromwell* we sit in our caravans, poring over the *Times* crossword, or in the luncheon marquee, sopping up the brandy while workmen strive to repair our lines of communication. The mud at least is authentic for the battle of Edgehill in which, as the Duke of Manchester, with the aid of a very slow horse, I am engaging the army of Charles I, or just possibly Charles II, so vague is my knowledge of history.

Normally I am not conscious of my weight, but I cannot help feeling a trifle guilty as the poor beast under me sinks slowly into the mire while we wait for clouds to pass. Even the director is puzzled, the last time he looked through the lens I was at least six inches taller. 'A cushion, perhaps?' he asks thoughtfully. 'Is there no way of jacking up the steed?' I am almost tempted to dismount and give back the money — almost, but not quite. Besides, I have several telling scenes later on which surely I shall be allowed to play on foot. But this film proves that from now on my cowboy roles are over. Not that I mind particularly. I am allergic to Westerns and actors leaning forward in the saddle to chat up the heroine. I shall leave all that to Richard Harris in this picture. But alas, in the role of Cromwell he seems to have little love-life. After shooting it's a different matter, of course. Richard, as gay as a cricket, is always off to Biarritz or San Sebastian. The rest of us stay soberly in Vittoria or Pamplona — well, perhaps soberly isn't quite the word, although most of us are at an age when we can carry our liquor, and few of the young seem to drink these days.

129

The hotel in Pamplona is to be preferred to the one in Vittoria, but on the other hand the latter has the Lamb Chop, a restaurant where you can eat with your fingers. 'Genuine Basque atmosphere,' we tell each other. The other attraction of the location is the leather factory. Everyone buys gear except me. If there's one thing I'm more uncomfortable on than a horse, it's a motorcycle. In the square in Pamplona I meet an old friend with whom I used to play poker in my youth. He lives these days in the town, and for the six days when they run the bulls. He has been gored twice. It's not the tips that do the damage, but the sides of the horns, apparently. The bulls are moving so fast that the flesh is burnt, and splits open. My friend runs for thirty seconds, the bulls for two and a half minutes. The whole thing takes place at six in the morning. If I'm still here I shall lock my bedroom door. I might, I suppose, join him outside the Cathedral on the evening before it all starts to watch the procession, when the bulls are blessed, in their absence, mercifully.

What an extraordinary country it is, and what an extraordinary man my friend has become. When he is not running for his life he is involved in the Carlist struggles about which little is heard outside Spain. When I first came to Cadiz long before the war, and during the days of the Republic, there was a curfew in all the big cities. Beggars made life intolerable in the cafés, and churches burnt fiercely. But now the beggars have disappeared and the church, risen from the ashes, is back again with a vengeance, and while there is no question of a curfew, British actors prefer to keep each other company in the evenings. The Spanish don't like us very much, although it pays them not to show it, at least by daylight. Perhaps, with all the fuss about Gibraltar, it's understandable, but why, I wonder, do I find them so unattractive, compared with my first impression all those years ago?

I have been to Spain a few times in the years between, but always in the south, and during the tourist season. Here in the north there are comparatively few foreign visitors, the economy is depressed and so are the inhabitants. I know the late Mr. Hemingway admired them inordinately, and they put up a statue to him in Pamplona outside his beloved bull-ring to prove it, but for my money they are a profoundly illiterate and superstitious nation, afraid to cross the street except where the policeman tells them to do so.

The University in Pamplona is one of the richest in the country. The students appear subdued, listless and compulsive yo-yo addicts. Have they retained this absurd toy all these years, or are we witnessing the birth of a new craze shortly to re-infect the whole of Europe? You cannot, my reader will expostulate, condemn a country on such trivial grounds as a fondness for yo-yos and pedestrian crossings. 'Didn't anything else strike you?' he will ask, and of course it did, but it's difficult to put into words, and in certain circumstances, for instance, if one was intending to buy a villa on the Costa Brava, it might be positively unwise. For this is a police state and as in all police states, whether they be Russia or Yugolslavia or even Hong Kong, the tourist senses the tension, and hugs it a little to himself. That man who spoke to us in the bar, why was he so anxious to know our opinion of the Generalissimo? The two men whispering in the dark little alley-way, the taxi driver who insists he speaks no English, yet drives with his ears cocked? Even the hall porter's demand for our passports occasions a not altogether unpleasurable frisson of apprehension. We cannot resist joining a little in the perpetual game of cops and robbers, but the Spaniard has played the game in earnest, and for more than thirty grim years.

Today the pace has by no means slackened. There is no let up, no guarantee that a man will be left alone to speak his mind. Small wonder that the Spaniard has grown silent, watchful and a little duller. It's not worth sticking out one's neck, it's wiser to do what the others do, to go to Mass, to walk in the square, to sit in the sun and when it sinks, in the little dark bars whiling away the time, watching football or the bullfights on the television, eating the occasional shrimp, waiting till it's time to go home to the wife at eleven o'clock and have dinner.

Except that dinner is a good deal later in Spain, is it after all so very different from what's happening in France or Italy, or even Great Britain? Under the Generalissimo there is better housing and health and education, even if wages are low and it takes a man a lifetime to save up enough money for a car. There's always the priest to tell him to take it easy, to prepare not for the family Scimitar, but for the life eternal. Spain is a Christian country, where Church and State march proudly hand in hand, and if they are followed at a respectful distance by little men in dark glasses who slink unobtrusively behind the pillars watching and listening, well after all, they too are priests, in a way, and anxious to hear a confession.

France and the French

During the First World War, the punishment for homosexuality in the French army was execution. However, if you were an officer you were allowed a final charge against the enemy, on the understanding that you got yourself shot. In one rather exceptional case the accused, who was the heir to enormous wealth and a proud title, was granted special leave from the battlefields until he had managed to consummate his marriage and procreate an heir. Eight months after he was killed in action, a child was born - a girl. That's the French for you — they take every trick but the last.

But for an Englishman there is always the fear that the French will win in the end. Every now and then one of my friends will put it to the test and retire with his ill-gotten gains to perch on one of those green-brown hills at the back of Cannes. But I am always struck by the sense of suspended animation which envelops him when he has acquired the sun blinds and the swimming pool. Once he has collected the sunshine and the gin, and of course the English papers, he is constantly obsessed with the price of butter.

My attitude to France was, I suppose, inherited from my father, who always felt perfectly at home there because he never attempted to talk or make friends with the natives. He admitted that there were certain things they did better than we did — sex and gambling, for instance — neither of which is true today. When I was sixteen and had left my last school, he decided that I should go into the Diplomatic Corps. He used to play bridge at his club with the Greek Ambassador, and usually won his money. 'They are a very decent class of fellow,' he told me. 'You'll enjoy being an Ambassador. Come on,' and having prized some money from his trustees, spirited me across the Channel to Tours, where he had been told the best French was spoken. Twenty-four hours in Tours shook him. He found himself encircled by the French. Hitherto he had always had

132

his back to the sea, and a good hall porter at his elbow. In Tours there wasn't even a good hotel.

'You don't care for this, surely?' he asked me. 'You wouldn't be happy here? There's nothing to do.'

'Learn French?' I asked him.

'Yes, but not here.' He was already fingering the money entrusted to him for my further education. We left for Monte Carlo that afternoon. 'This will be better for you,' my father assured me. 'You get all nationalities here. In the Diplomatic Service you'll find you have to mix.' My parent was anxious not to leave me alone with the wrong ambiance. Ambiance was one of his four French words. His other three were Le Bon Dieu.

'I believe,' he would reiterate, 'in Le Bon Dieu, which is why I find the Church of England service so frustrating.'

'You never go,' my mother told him.

'That is why,' he told her. 'Le Bon Dieu is everywhere except in an English church.' There was no arguing with Father, while the money lasted, at any rate. In Monte Carlo it didn't last very long, about ten days, and we were posting breathlessly home before the cheques bounced. In France it was an offence for cheques to bounce, and Father dreaded not arrest, but banishment from the casinos.

I myself was arrested in France when I was eight years old. I had swung a fishing line off the jetty and caught the hook in my thumb. I was led away by a gendarme, with blood streaming from my hand. As he marched me through the streets I sobbed, not with pain, but with terror. True, he took me to a doctor, and not the police station, but why didn't the fool tell me what he was doing? An English Bobby would have given me a toffee and told me I was a brave little chap. The French are a logical people, which is one reason the English dislike them so intensely. The other is that they own France, a country which we have always judged to be much too good for them. France has for centuries blocked our way to Europe. Before the invention of the aeroplane, we had to step over them to get anywhere. I was particularly conscious of this geographical fact as a child, because I lived at Folkestone, where the Channel is at its narrowest, and the packet sailed daily for Boulogne. When the gales blew, my nurse used to take me down to the Harbour to watch the homecoming passengers staggering down the gangplank, and crawling across the cobblestones to the Pavilion Hotel for a steadyer. 'Serve them right,' she would tell me. 'That's what you get for going abroad, Master Robert.' Intolerance was one of the subjects she taught me in the nursery, and I was a willing pupil.

For me intolerance is still the adrenalin in the vein of society. Without it we should perish, with it we get into trouble. The intolerance of white to black, Gentile to Jew, rich to poor, and vice versa makes for battle, murder and sudden death. It also keeps everyone who stays alive fighting fit for a short time. In the intolerance league, the British are still top — an unaccustomed position for this old country these days. Over the years we have hung labels round the necks of foreigners. Americans are brash, Spaniards lazy, Germans gross, Turks treacherous, Russians dangerous and the Italians pathetic. We suffer them to live in their own lands only because they have to be there to be ready to fetch and carry for us when we have our holidays.

It is this concept of the British as the absentee landlords of the world that has served us so splendidly in the past, but it is one that the French have never accepted. They persist in believing that France belongs to them. The argument has been going on for some centuries. At various times in our history we have had to resort to fisticuffs, and one day no doubt we shall have to do so again. But it would be foolish not to recognise that the present is a period of stalemate, and there is little we can do just at the moment but pay up and look pleasant. We don't like paying bills any more than the French do, but at least we struggle to do so. When De Gaulle died, his epitaph was spoken by the landlord of my local inn. 'I'm sorry the old chap's gone, but he never paid the bill for Dunkirk, did he?'

Another fact I learned in my nursery was that the Frogs were a violent lot. In those days every revue, and most musical comedies, contained an Apache Number, in which a French Cad in sidewhiskers and a tight fitting black suit assaulted a girl in slow tempo around the stage. The girl wore, as we believed all Frenchwomen did, a slit skirt, and had her hair pulled a good deal before being finally knocked down, rolled over and abandoned. She would lie unconscious on the floor until resuscitated by her partner for the curtain call.

Years later I had my earlier impression of the French confirmed, while staying in the Rue de Rivoli. The Rue de Rivoli, as most readers probably know already, is an absurdly long colonnaded street, running from the Place de la Concorde to the Louvre, and a good way beyond. For a time when I was making a picture in Paris, I lived at the Hotel Brighton, and had a bedroom overlooking the Tuileries Gardens. In the evening, after a day's shooting, I would repair to the bar and sit watching the television before dinner. If it was raining, and it usually seemed to be, I would then walk under cover to a restaurant in the Place Vendôme.

134

One evening, as I stepped into the Arcade, I saw at a distance of two hundred yards, a man carrying a body emerge from a lighted doorway and crossing the pavement, attack the colonnade with his victim's head. Half a dozen times he swung his human battering ram, and then casually abandoning it, let what was left of it fall into the gutter, and returned to the bistro. I suppose I could have arrived on the scene quicker, but when I did, the horror and fright I felt had been replaced by righteous indignation. With scarcely a glance at the crumpled corpse, I tore into the café and into the half a dozen silent, sulky Frenchmen who sat there. A torrent of pidgin French, stage argot and half-remembered phrases from the Folies Bergères poured from my lips.

'Bêtes sauvages! Canaille! Méchants hommes! Quelle bêtise, quelle exposition formidable! Que va dire Le General? Appellez les gendarmes!' I looked round for the man who had committed the crime, but could not identify him, yet they had all been there. They had watched, they had done nothing, and now a man lay dead in the gutter, and still no one moved.

'Ambulance!' I shouted, 'Appellez un ambulance, vite, vite! Very well, if you won't do it, I shall.' I seized the telephone, and realised I hadn't the slightest idea how to proceed. I pushed the receiver into the hands of the one I took to be the proprietor. 'Appellez,' I ordered. 'Appellez, vite! Pas de nonsense! Attendez!'

I really had them mesmerised. I think in that brief instant I realised why it is Englishmen are so good in a crisis. Slow to anger, perhaps, but when we are aroused our fury is really magnificent. 'Venez!' I reiterated, 'venez, vite!' and for the first time employing physical force, drove my finger deep into the patron's chest. There was a hint of menace now in the way in which he replaced the receiver on its stand. His eyes were fixed on something at the back of me. I spun round, ready for a surprise attack, to find the corpse had now got to his feet and was dusting himself off. Then he started to laugh. I can never forgive him that laugh. I like to think he was concussed, but I can never be sure. All I know is I had to pay for the telephone call before I could leave the bistro.

But at least on that occasion I didn't have a Frenchman on my side. The French are never on anyone's side for very long. When they capitulated in 1941, the general feeling in my country was that at last we could get on and win the war. 'Now we know where we are,' we told each other. I was making another picture at the time, and the mood in the studio when we heard that Paris had fallen was one of quiet optimism. Only the director was silent and apprehensive.

135

'Come,' I said to him at luncheon, 'surely the rushes can't have been all that terrible. No worse than yesterday's, at least.'

'It's not the rushes for once,' he told me. 'It's Paris. You wouldn't understand what Paris means to me. It's the last place left in Europe where one can purchase genuine chamois leather gloves, buttoning to the armpits.'

I imagine if chamois leather gloves are being stitched these days, the British have the monopoly. It is curious how the pole of sexual permissiveness has shifted. Now it is the French who are the Puritans and we the libertines. A friend of mine, who recently had a few hours to kill in Nice, decided to spend them in a brothel. Being a writer, the word bordello came eventually to his lips and his need manifested itself to the hall porter of the hotel in which he was lodged. He was directed to an apartment on the Front, and in the parlour explained to the proprietress that what he enjoyed most was a sound whipping. A moment later and he was back on the Promenade des Anglais, Madame's rebuke still ringing in his ears: 'Pardon, Monsieur, c'est une maison serieuse.'

'Of course,' he told me when he recounted the incident, 'I may not have made myself understood.'

It's always a mistake trying to speak French to the Frogs. As Noel Coward once remarked when he was sustaining a role at the Comédie Française, 'They simply don't understand their own langue.' How true. 'Place de la Concorde,' you say to the taxi driver, and he sits uncomprehending while you repeat your instructions a dozen times before he consents to shrug his shoulders and get going. Once he has secured you as his passenger, he will take his time before deciding on the destination. 'Place de la Concorde,' he will suddenly announce, braking abruptly, and turning the cab round come scuttling back from the Bois de Boulogne, where he has been enjoying a skelter at your expense. In England a taxi driver doesn't make the foreigner pronounce Waterloo twenty-seven times before conveying him to the railway station. He doesn't have to. He knows he's going to miss the boat train anyway, because of the traffic jam.

The French and Ourselves these days both keep boarding-houses. Our windows face each other, but whereas there is usually a sign hanging up in our front parlour advertising vacancies, the French always seem to be Complet. When an American rings the bell over the road, the door is opened immediately. There is little fuss, hardly any formality, no questions asked. He just signs the book and pays up. Naturally, we on this side expect him to pay up, but before doing so there are a whole lot of questions to be answered. Is he

136

respectable? How long will he be staying? Whom are we to notify if he dies? What is his purpose in coming? Was his mother an Armenian? We don't mind if she was, but we like to know.

Every year, little pieces of the white cliffs of Dover crumble away and fall into the Channel, which you might think would have the effect of increasing the distance between our coast lines, yet today the French stand nearer to us than ever, and with the Hovercraft service, a projected Channel Tunnel and the Common Market, we seem to be in danger of actually touching. It will not be an easy embrace, if I have my way.

The other day, deciding to find out for myself how real is the danger of a final clinch, I bought a ticket on a Hovercraft, a vehicle of which I have always been slightly ashamed, believing it to be another British invention which failed to jell, and imagining the South Coast of my beautiful land littered with these rusting giants, and set sail for Boulogne. True, when I came upon it in Dover, it was stranded, apparently helpless on the sand, but a spirit of optimism prevailed among its attendants. Concrete ramps had been constructed leading to the doors of the monster and soon passengers were being invited to climb on board. I found the loading procedure unnerving. Care has to be taken lest the thing should tip sideways, and when I stepped on to the port side, two other passengers were hastily urged forward on the starboard deck. Hovercrafts apparently cannot decide whether they are boats or planes. Lifebelts are circular, but on the other hand there are air hostesses, young ladies with bossy manners in identical uniforms, barking instructions and soliciting orders for duty-free demon alcohol and Customs-exempt cancer sticks. For those of us who have never worked on the roads, Hovercraft travel is perhaps the nearest they will get to operating a pneumatic compressor. Once aloft, they are not, of course, grasping it by the handle, but actually bouncing up and down in the saddle. Sucking up a gin and tonic through a straw — conveying a glass to my lips nearly knocked my teeth out — I learnt that the fellow in the next jump seat was paying his first visit to France. He was planning to return that evening, reckoning he would be able to see all he wanted to of 'abroad' in six hours, provided he wasn't poisoned by the grub.

My own plans called for a rather longer visit. I didn't propose to return for twenty-four hours, just in time to scuttle through my stage door on Monday night in time to receive the customers. Visiting France while one is acting in the London theatre always adds excitement to the trip. I have never yet been posted as a defaulter, but there's always a first time. The nearest I ever came to it was when

David Tomlinson flew me to Le Touquet, and on the way home his engine started to cough. On that occasion I wasn't worried so much about missing a single performance, but the rest of the run.

Boulogne served in the war as a bomb dump for returning allied missions who had failed to locate their intended target further inland. It has been rebuilt with both eyes on the car ferry. I was reminded of a Christmas toy for eight-year-olds. The nursery floor is covered with sections of motorway, some of it not yet assembled. Stepping out, except along the promenade, is unattractive and dangerous.

The French cannot bear to look out through a restaurant window without being able to read the price of the crustacea and coq au vin they are consuming, in reverse. They insist on being constantly reminded of the cost of living expressed in rump steak and chips. The only thing that makes us British suspicious lest the French have more of the stuff than we have, is they never think of anything else. A nation always ready to put its hand in anyone's pocket except its own. I chose a bistro where I could glimpse the sea between the lines of graffiti, and after lunch joined the proprietor and his friends for a discussion on the Common Market. Everyone agreed that it was in our interest to join. Meanwhile it was in their interest to pop over on the Hovercraft and shop in Dover.

After luncheon I took a taxi and drove over to Le Touquet. In the Casino, in the vast hotels, on the deserted plage, nothing stirred. For most of the year Le Touquet is a ghost town, only coming to life for a few short weeks in the high summer. Out of season its mood is set by the shells of the great hotels standing derelict in the forest, like the ruins of Ankhor Vat. Legend has it that Le Touquet died just as the war was ending, the result of a drunken escapade by four American airmen who wanted a little action. If you want action these days, Le Touquet is the last place in which to find it. Perhaps the French never intended to rebuild it. Perhaps they didn't want to be reminded of the English milords who patronised the place between the wars, accepting that in any case they wouldn't come back even if they could afford to. Those stuffed shirts who cried 'Garçon!' and 'Banco!', and competed on the golf links and polo grounds for perpetual challenge cups given by English clubs and British regiments, and presented personally to the victors by the Prince of Wales or Gladys Cooper. In those days we actors used to queue up at the barrier at Victoria Station on Sunday mornings to catch the boat train with our share of the week's booty, anxious to join our betters on the green turf or across the green baize. We were bound for a continent to which we British have never really belonged, but which in those days we really believed belonged to us.

It was dark when I returned to Boulogne. The ferry had stopped running, the waterfront was deserted. I had dinner in the empty hotel dining-room, and went to bed. In the morning when I got into the bath there was no soap. When I stepped out of it, there was no towel. I rang the bell, and no one came. Eventually, to stop myself shivering I dried myself on a sheet, calculating how much the French must have saved themselves over the years by not providing their customers with soap or bath towels.

Nowadays they don't even come when the customer calls. They surely can't imagine that it's our turn to answer the bell?

It Is Better To Travel Hopefully . . .

Somewhere in the pocket of one of my suits is an advertisement for the Pakistani Airline. I have an idea their address is in Regent Street, and I have walked up and down past Hamley's and Mappin & Webb, searching for it lately. Why on earth don't I find the page or look it up in the telephone book? The answer is I don't really want to set out immediately for Katmandu. It is in the nature of a project. One of my many projects, like my visit to China, my stay in Bolivia, temporarily shelved after reading about the place in a Sunday supplement, or my insistence on seeing Naples again before I die, but meanwhile, and just for the moment, I am still hanging around Shaftesbury Avenue, lying low, waiting for the break. This is the time of the year when I cross the road to look in the windows of travel agents, but it's not a holiday I am seeking. I am not attracted by the gay poster or the cheap inclusive rate, with the individual shower and balcony. I yearn for sterner pleasures. In the Earls Court Road there are notice boards offering the most exhausting experiences. 'Small mixed party proceeding overland to the Upper Amazon have vacancy for spare driver. Bivouac-style accommodation, own sleeping bag essential.' I dream of joining a student group intent on studying primitive life in the lower Sudan, but fear rejection.

No, when I do set off I shall travel alone, as usual. It's not speed I'm after, but avoiding embarrassment. The truth is I don't really like other people to watch me en route. I am a slut where sightseeing is concerned. I have no particular love of churches. I dislike the castles and palaces once they have been gutted of treasure. I don't care for history unless it's quirky. On a hill outside Lebanon I searched for and found the grave of Lady Hester Stanhope, and later chided our ambassador in Beirut that it was neglected. I had been attracted to the tomb by a sentence in a guide book. 'Finally abandoned by the Sheiks, she took to the hills and the study of sorcery.' She who had

140

once ruled England, or at least had advised her uncle on how it should be run, ended up in the wilderness, brewing up bats' wings. It's not how they start, but how they finish that interests me.

I hate shattered sculpture, ruined forts. I love camel markets and bazaars. I like noise and filth and stench. I detest the smell of incense burning in empty cathedrals or full ones either, for that matter. I get no kick from a twelfth-century reredos. I am not the stuff of which Kenneth Clark is made.

Arriving in a new place, I am invariably disappointed. This is not how I pictured Samarkand, I tell myself. The truth is, of course, I never pictured it at all. As soon as I arrive, I want to be off. I find the harbour or the bus station, and read the destination boards. If the lettering is indecipherable, so much the better. I hop on the coach and pretend I know where I'm going, pay the conductor the same amount as the man who sits beside me, alight where he alights, and wonder what the hell I'm going to do in a hillside slum for three hours before the bus returns. But I find something, even if it's only to sit in the café in the square, and if possible in the sun. I watch nothing whatever happening, and am content. On the way back I grab the seat next to the window and am disappointed that the route is familiar.

In Belgrade there never seemed more than one way out of the town. I chose the bigger bus, always hoping to get further. One evening I found myself back at Munich. Another time I reached Kotor after a hell of a journey and rang up to see if they had missed me on the film I was making. They had. 'Come back,' they urged, 'all is forgiven.' It had taken me three days to arrive, but the guide-book insisted Belgrade could be reached from Kotor in four hours by a new crack express operating on the recently-built line linking the capital with the Mediterranean.

'Get me a first class ticket,' I urged the porter.

'On what?' he asked.

'The train, the express, the Trans-Yugoslavian Queen.'

'There is no such thing,' he told me.

I showed him the guide-book. 'Very well,' I said, 'book me by the slow train.'

But he seemed unimpressed. 'There is no line,' he replied. In the end I commandeered the light aeroplane which transported the mail. I used up a lot of stamps, but of course no one got their letters for a week.

In Istanbul, boats are always leaving the quay. The game is played by rushing up the gangway at the last moment, and then starting to worry in case one is bound for Australia and not just another island in the Sea of Marmora. Why all this rushing around, Morley? Why can't you keep still, stay put? Heaven knows, you're old enough. To me it's awful to have lived sixty-odd years on an earth which I haven't seen properly. Geographically, I don't suppose there are any more surprises. I have taken in sea coasts with palms and sea coasts with mountains and sea coasts with houses. I have driven across deserts and through country lanes, along American highways and Turkish mule tracks. I have pottered in Hong Kong and Huddersfield. They are different, of course, but not all that different. The cities and the plains of the world are the same basically, but it's the people living in them who vary. The maids bathing fully dressed in the Bosphorus; Japanese ladies exchanging gift-wrapped sugar at the Tokyo Hilton; the trussed live crabs with bass in Macao; Sinatra in Vegas. In Istanbul I found a bear trained as a masseur. How I longed to bring him home with me and set him up in business on some shady Soho landing. I would have pinned a card to the bell push; 'Bear Massage', and waited for the terrified customers to remonstrate over the spelling. I always like to have the last laugh. I must really go through my suits again, and find that address.

MORLEY
AT
LARGE

How Common Is The Market?

'I should like,' I told them, 'to make up my mind about the Common Market.'

'You've done that already,' they said.

'I could be wrong. I'd better go and have another peek.'

'Deauville?'

'Deauville!'

'I should have thought,' they observed, 'you would have done better to have tried Brussels.'

But Brussels is not by the sea, nor has it as yet a casino. If one is to observe the Common Market, one should surely look on the bright side. When I was first told about the Common Market, I believed like most of my fellow countrymen we were being given what we are always looking for, something for nothing, or at least for very little: a small investment in the pools to produce the treble chance dividend. For years people like myself had misjudged the foreigners; all the time all they wanted was to share with us. But to share what?

Well, for a start the seaside, after all it's their seaside we know best. Long tired of our own, of the boring drive, the boring weather and the boredom when we get there, we have of recent years treated ourselves to the Costa Brava, the Costa del Sol and all the other Costas. So much prettier sounding and looking, too, than Bognor and Weston-Super-Mare. It wasn't only the sunshine which made continental holidays so appealing, it was, as we kept murmuring to each other, the ambiance, a simple word which we learnt to pronounce rather cockily. We also learnt to ask for certain foods and drinks native to the natives. Pizzas, Spaghetti Bolognese, Vino, Frutta Del Mare. If we craved more nourishing food such as fish and chips, our hosts supplied it, at a price which relentlessly increased year by year.

But this year was the first year we ceased to be guests and became partners, and life would surely be cheaper for partners, or so we believed. I can only report that in Deauville, alas, life is still very, expensive indeed. A hotel bedroom costs twenty pounds a night, breakfast mercifully included, but the mercy stops abruptly once you get to the plage. The bathing pool costs a pound, a tent on the sands two pounds, luncheon en plein air, which is free, can be had for five pounds. If, tiring of such extravagance, you desire a taxi to drive the few hundred yards back to the hotel, the journey cannot be accomplished for less than another pound, so that after paying for your bedroom and before paying for your tea, you have spent by anyone's reckoning twenty-eight pounds, and should you decide to return to the pool after your siesta and dine modestly in a bistro, the day's expenditure on the simple life leaves you forty pounds the poorer.

Supposing yourself to be a family man, accompanied by your brood, a week at the seaside in France with trimmings can scarcely be had for less than five hundred pounds. How on earth, you ask yourself, do the French manage it, for let it be said straight away that there are no English this year in Deauville, and not likely to be any by all accounts, to use the operative word. When we say no English people, there will of course be the usual crowd for the Grande Semaine, but these are the very old, the very rich and the simply daring. Such international funsters are not the stuff of which package deals are composed; they seldom dig castles on the sands. Why should they? After all, they already have castles.

But to return to the French, who are at Deauville in quite large numbers; are they then richer than we? Can they afford the prices? The answer, as is so often the case, is yes and no. They are richer, but they can't, except in rare instances, afford their own prices. How then do they manage? Not to understand how the French manage and propose to go on managing, is the cardinal miscalculation of our government. Just as Hitler announced his plans in advance and nobody bothered to read *Mein Kampf,* so the Europeans and especially the French, announced their plans, but you won't find a single copy of the Treaty of Rome for sale anywhere in Deauville.

At least *Mein Kampf* sold a few copies and stayed on the bookstalls. What escaped me, and less surprisingly the Treasury officials, was that the French never spoke of a Common Market at all; they spoke of the European Economic Community, the key word being right there in the middle. Economy is the thing the French really understand. There has never been a nation more dedicated to the art of not spending a bean. The French themselves don't stay in the hotels along the front, nor do they bathe in the swimming pool or hire tents and Bath chairs. They don't ride in taxis, they don't eat in restaurants, they don't drink in the cafés, save for an occasional small cup of coffee or a glass of beer, and then usually Mother and the children content themselves with sniffing Father's cup and eating Father's lump sugar. To watch a Frenchman pay for something is to watch him die a slow death. Car payer, c'est mourir un peu. A French purse has around it a guard ensuring that not one sou escapes.

In front of me in the queue there stood a man convinced he was being overcharged for a rail ticket to Paris. He argued, cajoled, appealed to all and sundry and effectively stopped several would-be passengers from catching the train. In the end nothing would satisfy him until the issuing official wrote his own name and the price extracted on each ticket for reference at a later date to the Minister of Transport with a view to a possible refund. This sort of thing simply couldn't happen on British Rail, where, since prices change almost hourly, there would seem to be more excuse. The French are a passionate race and their passion is and always will be, money. They are the dedicated tightwads of the world, travelling in the baggage car and arriving at the destination at the same time as the first-class passengers in their wagon lits. They may not have had a very comfortable journey, but they are all the better off because of it.

To argue that theirs is a false economy is to waste not only their time, but ours. We can't beat them, but whoever suggested we might join them is out of his tiny mind.

France today is a vast clip joint, and clip joints are by tradition sparsely patronised. The French waiter stands by the empty tables and flicks invisible specks of dust off the empty chairs. The bathing pool built for a thousand is patronised by less than fifty, the car parks are empty. The cars temporarily abandoned by their owners are a long walk from the sands, but Maman and Papa, petit Jean and his beau-mère, petite Justine, petit Auguste and le chien alight from them and march beachwards, their chairs, their picnic, their parasol, their set of boules, their wine, their inflatable raft, their scuba outfit, their fishing rods, their cameras and their tape recorder, their towels and bathing suits borne aloft. It's a good deal to carry, but they are a happy band of warriors; not one of them is spending a sausage. The shopkeepers, the barmen, the waiters, the hotel porters, the bathing pool attendants, stand idly outside their respective establishments and watch them pass in grudging admiration. A Frenchman would always rather put up his shutters than bring down his prices, it's in his blood.

An empty people, living empty lives in an empty land. The old men of Europe doze fitfully, Pompidou, Franco, Caetano, Brandt. Partners? Sleeping partners perhaps, but not for long, surely?

By the way, there is something very wrong with the second roulette wheel on the right as you enter the salle privée in the Casino Municipale.

Surgical Spirit

It was one of my 'bilious days'. As a child I used to have them at regular intervals. 'Come here,' Doctor Farr ordered. I rose from the sofa where I habitually spent bilious days, and tottered to the dining-room table still covered with a white cloth. Doctor Farr used it to demonstrate his problem and mine. He drew a small circle in pencil. 'This, boy,' he announced, 'is the size of your tummy, and this,' now he drew a much larger circle, 'is what you persist in trying to cram into it.' I am still incensed when I recall his diagnosis. Even allowing for the fact that medicine, like myself, was in its infancy at that time, he should have realised that such a brutal statement was likely to offend such an artistic, delicate child as myself. It would have served him right if from then on I had patronised the pharmacist, not the doctor.

Fortunately for the medical profession I still prefer to wait in the consulting-room, rather than the chemist's. I don't, of course, relish the dingy grandeur of Harley Street. I am depressed by large central tables and dog-eared copies of *Punch*. Sitting round with other patient patients, I think how much nicer it would be if we were actually invited to a meal in the room in which we now all sit equidistant from the polished mahogany and on our reproduction Hepplewhite seats.

What happens, we wonder, at closing time? Are the magazines tidied away, the gilt horses taken from over the fireplace, to serve as a centrepiece for the richly-laden table? Do the doctors' families feast here together, and if so are they attired in Victorian dress to match the furniture and the drapes, or is it all pretence, and does each doctor, cash-box under arm, creep stealthily down the stairs from his consulting-room, to sit round the table with his colleagues, sharing out the booty? Is there, in the manner of casinos, a *chef de partie*, supervising the counting of the petty cash when the table closes? The

149

truth is, I suppose, that everyone gets out fast and that few doctors care to linger in their own waiting-rooms, where anxiety clings like cigar smoke to the pelmets.

There is a lot to be said for the country surgery which I patronise. For one thing it is always full of babies attending for their jabs, and for another both partners employ a phrase in consultation of which I am particularly fond, and which I always find immensely reassuring. Whether it is pink-eye, incipient tonsillitis, an ingrowing toenail or high blood pressure from which I believe myself to be suffering, they allay my anxiety with the simple statement that there is a lot of it about. I find it so comforting to realise that most of the inhabitants of my village, and all the babies, are currently fighting the same dread symptoms.

Actors who accept film engagements have, like racehorses when they come under the hammer, to submit to a medical examination. There is nothing I dread more. The questionnaire which precedes the examination is fiendish, the weighing and measuring an affront to human dignity. The very idea of having my blood pressure taken sends it sky high, and when the ceremony actually takes place, I am aware only of my pounding heart and the startled expression on the face of the apparatus. By the time the ritual beaker is presented, I am a prey to the final anxiety. Ah, the relief of filling the goblet to the brim!

On the operating table, on the other hand, I am comparatively calm, telling myself that with modern techniques and apparatus there are few places where a man is safer. Should anything stop on the work bench, it is a comparatively easy matter to start it up again. The spanners and blow-torch are to hand, to say nothing of the increasing spares which hospitals carry these days. My own operational experiences have been on the whole enjoyable. To have subjected oneself to the knife is still regarded by family and friends as something of an achievement. Once the operation is over, there is a definite scent of courage mixing pleasantly with that of the surgical spirit. Beside being able to boast of one's own sangfroid, one can and one does pay tribute to the chap who actually did the job. Surgeons, like schoolmasters and portrait painters, are on a shilling to nothing before they start. However atrocious their manners, however inept their execution, they cannot be judged by us ordinary mortals. We are prone to praise our surgeon extravagantly without the slightest knowledge of the form. If he stays too long at our bedside, it is we who are to blame should the conversation flag. If his manner is brisk, even brusque, and his visit fleeting, we remind ourselves of how busy he is saving other lives besides our own.

150

Once, believing myself to be recovering from major surgery, I pressed my surgeon to drop by one evening for a chat. I hinted that there was so much about his own life that fascinated and enthralled me. I pointed out that, having afforded him the opportunity of exploring my guts, the least he could do would be to let me have similar facilities with regard to his libido. For some reason he took me at my word, at four o'clock one morning. I opened my eyes to find him sitting by my bedside, and realised I was dying. In vain he protested there was nothing amiss, that he had been on his way home from an emergency call and had dropped by on the chance I was awake. 'Alive, you mean,' I told him, and demanded to know the exact nature of the complications which I was convinced had now arisen. Was it my breathing, my heart, my brain which was about to pack up? When he finally took his leave, we had not mentioned his libido. My own, however, has never fully recovered.

Hugo, Or Back to the Crawling Board

Slumped in our chairs, Hugo and I were spending the afternoon on the lawn. Time was when we would both have napped, but my grandson has passed the age for sleeping in the afternoon, whereas for me the habit becomes more and more compelling. But now, alas, a sense of duty prevented me from nodding off. Hugo seemed in no immediate danger, as he presently climbed from his chair and started to crawl around, searching for daisies, a diet of which he never seems to tire. He reminded me, as I watched him savouring their subtle flavour, of some dedicated oyster fancier.

'Now that you have been with us nearly a year,' I said, 'have you formed any general impression of our predicament?' I did not expect an answer. I spoke merely to distract his attention from the feast. There is a theory, propounded no doubt by Dr. Spock, that too many are bad for the appetite. I was surprised, therefore, when, having considered my question, he answered it, at the same time carefully expelling the beard of a flower.

'It's curious you should ask me that. I was pondering the matter in the early hours of the morning, while awaiting my orange juice. How late you all sleep, to be sure. Are you referring to your personal predicament as an ageing comedian, or to the state of the human race as a whole?'

'Both,' I told him.

'You must understand,' said my grandson, 'that before one was born nearly a year ago, one was briefed in general terms as to what to expect, and indeed what would be expected of one. There are available to those about to be born all the latest baby books, and droll reading most of us find it, I can tell you. Not that one doesn't occasionally get ideas from them, but besides them one has lectures on the crisis days. A new-born babe, you understand, dreads two things — precipitation and confrontation. He has a morbid fear of being dropped, and a reluctance to accept his parents at first sight. A lot of babies imagine that the doctor who delivers them is a parent, and are often bitterly disappointed when introduced to their actual fathers, and indeed refuse to accept them for some time, and on occasions permanently. On the other hand, they nearly always seem to settle for the mother. They are a pretty adaptable lot on the whole. What was it Tennyson wrote? 'Ours not to reason why'? In any case, we are all sworn to silence for at least a year, and then there's a general agreement not to say anything significant for some time afterwards. As soon as we start to talk we go back to square one. We have to learn to grope around with the rest of you in the dark.'

'Before the light goes out, is there any help you could give, any advice you care to offer?'

'About yourself? A good deal. For instance, I never understand why you *read* the papers.'

'What would you do?'

'Tear them up. Haven't you noticed, I always tear up newspapers? That's the only possible satisfaction to be got out of them. It's not as if you were interested in what's going on around you.'

'What do you mean? I'm passionately interested.'

'In the theatrical gossip, perhaps, but famine in India, earthquakes in Persia, fighting in Nigeria — despite them you still eat a hearty breakfast, slumber on the lawn. Nothing shakes you. Tell me, when was the last time you ate a daisy?'

'I don't happen to like daisies, but I suppose I munched a few of them when I was your age.'

'They taste quite different,' Hugo assured me. 'They've entirely changed the flavour of daisies. And the grass, don't you notice the grass is a different colour? And the trees, how tall they are now-adays. When did you last chew a lump of coal, or pull the pile from a carpet, or bite on a door? When did you last sprinkle milk, or choke on a rusk, or dip your fingers in custard? You see, you're really not alive at all. You don't do any of the exciting things. You just sit there, oblivious of your surroundings, missing all the fun. Why don't you crawl over there to the path, and try sucking a pebble?'

I felt rather foolish, but the pebble was cool, and not at all unpleasant.

'There's a clever boy, then,' said Hugo, joining me on the gravel. 'Be careful you don't swallow it.'

'You were going to give me some advice,' I reminded him.

'I have just done so. The trouble with you, Grandfather Robert, is

153

a basic lack of perception. You have discarded your own senses in favour of instant touch, instant smell, instant taste. You glance, you never gaze, hear but you never listen. What you need is a refresher course in babyhood. Back to the crawling board.'

Suddenly I saw it — a vast building, perhaps in Bond Street next door to Elizabeth Arden, where men of my age would be lifted out of their executive Bentleys and carried screaming across the threshold, to be plonked down on a giant-sized nursery rug, and encouraged to crawl one step at a time up an enormous staircase to the giant playroom, where great blocks of plywood, decorated with lead-free paint, were waiting to be piled on top of one another, and where teddy bears as large as themselves were ready to be bitten and sucked, and have their button eyes gouged out. At mealtimes, too, what pleasures would lie in store for the customers. To taste tapioca and jelly again, to be fed, from the giant economy size tins, sieved bacon and egg with added cereal breakfast, grated mutton, carrot and custard lunch, and genuine hip syrup rusks for tea. A crash course of babyhood to attract all the more go-ahead tycoons. A fortune was in my lap, and all I had to do was grasp it. 'Hugo,' I cried, opening my eyes, 'how can I ever thank you?' But Hugo had disappeared. Panic seized me. I scanned the lawn, then started up and began a guilty search. How could I have been so lacking in grandparental sense of duty? 'Hugo! Hugo!' I cried. 'Where are you?', and came upon him suddenly under a gooseberry bush. 'You haven't eaten one? They're not ripe.'

Hugo didn't answer. I sensed he was back to square one. In his eyes there was a look of pity. 'Where did you expect to find me?' he seemed to be asking.

The Super Seven

When I have to die, I should like to do so in the foyer of the best hotel in the world. For one thing I feel most confident in hotel foyers, and for another, disposing of my corpse would be a final test for the Hall Porter. I have always been a snob about hotels — about people too, I suppose, but that need not concern us. For me the best hotel in whatever place I happen to be, is a must. Ensconced in any other establishment, I tend to sulk. Once, on the steamer to Capri, I was examining the luggage tags of one of the most beautiful girls I have ever seen, when I discovered to my dismay that she was bound for a different hotel from the one I had selected. I decided there and then to adjust my itinerary, to stay where she stayed. Yet it was not the child's beauty that prompted my action, but the obvious wealth of her companion. He was, I decided, an Indian princeling, and as such, could be relied upon. When we landed, I followed hard on their heels, up the mountain to Annacapri and through the revolving doors of their Shangri-La, only to be dismissed by an obdurate reception clerk. Forced to return to the hotel of my original choice, I spent my holiday in jealous despair.

Each new hotel has for me the excitement of an untried mistress. I am impatient with the preliminaries, eager to register, and afterwards to rid myself of the attentions of the bell-hop who has preceded me with my key along the corridor, and unlocked my room. I watch him demonstrating the central heating, the public address system, the television remote controls, and long for the moment when he will withdraw and leave me in possession. I know from experience it will be a considerable time before my luggage arrives, and meanwhile my room and I will be getting to know one another. As soon as the bell-hop collects his fee and withdraws, I hurry into the bathroom to inspect the plumbing, to admire the tumblers wrapped in cellophane and the lavatory pan decorated as if for a marriage. Is there a bidet?

155

How large are the soap tablets? How many towels? Flannels? Gift samples? I test the heat of the towel rail, the noise of the toilet flush, make sure I understand how the taps function. These grow more complicated with every year. I am particularly fond of the built-in thermometer, although I can never remember the exact temperature at which I prefer to bathe.

I hurry back into the bedroom itself to inspect the thickness of the drapes, the pile of the carpet. I adjust the lights, toy with the television, take in the view. This is the moment of truth, and I must ask myself whether this is really the best bedroom I can expect — for the price. Am I on the right side, at the right height? Do I want to look out over the swimming pool, or the garage? Now is the time for action, if I decide to change. I must pick up the phone, demand to be connected to the desk clerk, get into the poker game, and be prepared if necessary to have him call my bluff.

My decision as to whether to accept the original accommodation proffered, or to try and improve on my hand, depends largely on the ambiance I have already encountered at the reception desk. I can usually tell whether I am being given the bum's rush. One day I will accept a small back room over the dustbins, on another even a penthouse suite is inadequate. Having decided to stay put, I start to explore the closets, paying particular attention to the way the doors are hung and the drawers slide. I assess the writing paper, read the breakfast menu, and the other brochures provided. I can never have too much of any of these. I like to know that I can write letters on all kinds of differently-shaped paper, and that there is a wide choice of breakfast cereals, bars and restaurants. I am always ready to sample Frosted Grape Nuts, to plan an evening in their Sapphire Room or the House of Genji, to have a cocktail in the Eagle's Nest or the Imperial Viking, a nightcap in Nero's Nook. On the whole I avoid coffee shops and grill rooms, believing that if a man takes the trouble to find a name, however bizarre, he may equally have taken the trouble to find a chef.

When eventually my luggage arrives, I am already unpacked. The actual disposing of my belongings becomes something of an anticlimax. I am conscious of the inadequacy of my wardrobe, beset with a longing for a hundred handkerchiefs, a thousand ties, a multitude of socks to fill every drawer, an infinity of suits to exhaust the coathangers.

I have always believed in myself as a world jurist where hotels are concerned. I still hope that even now in the afternoon, the early afternoon, of my life, I may be invited to become one. How pleasant

156

it would be to travel the world in the company of a few others like myself, sampling the delights and extravagances provided by great hoteliers, and to award the annual ROBERTS. There would have to be several, naturally. For the hotel which had the best cellar, the hotel with the best plumbing, the one with the best hall porter. The best hotel built in the last year. The hotel with the most beautiful setting, or simply the most beautiful hotel. If actresses are entitled to Oscars, why not hotels? The latter are more exciting, more unpredictable, and with notable exceptions, better behaved. Moreover hotels, except those in the very top class have, like film stars, to show off. I am never intimidated by ostentation; being in the business myself, I understand it.

Once, staying in a hotel in Fez, where the uniforms of the staff were the most magnificent I have ever encountered, I approached a lackey even more gorgeously attired than the bell-boys, whom I imagined to be the hall porter, with some trivial request about procuring a fleet of camels for the afternoon.

'I think you are making a mistake,' remarked my accosted, 'I have the honour to be the personal aide de camp to His Majesty the King of Libya.' I shook him warmly by the hand, but did not apologise.

In selecting what are in my opinion the seven great hotels of the world I am tempted to include this beautiful Moroccan Caravanserai, but things I am told have changed in Morocco since I was there; besides, a simultaneous visit of myself and the King of Libya may have ensured an unnatural and temporary standard of excellence. An even more potent reason for not including it in my list is that I have entirely forgotten its name.

I am not in favour of the Award Committee, when it is formed, arriving anywhere incognito. Let us see the *best* you can do — not the worst, should be our admonition. Personally I am careful, when arriving at any hotel where I suspect I may — initially at least — be unrecognised, to employ a gamesmanship ploy of which I and not Stephen Potter am the inventor. 'I think,' I remark casually, leaning across the reception desk and addressing the clerk, 'you may be expecting me. My secretary has made the reservation: ROBERT MORLEY.' I speak the last two words slowly and loudly. The impression I wish to give is that I am far too modest to believe that the name will mean anything to him; and if as sometimes happens the idiot hasn't in fact heard of me he will begin to check his list.

'Nothing here,' he will not unnaturally remark when he has done so.

I take care to appear thunderstruck. 'Are you quite certain? My

157

secretary has been with me a number of years and this is the first time anything like this has happened.'

After this I play it by ear; if, as sometimes, there is plenty of accommodation available I like to believe that I will be offered something a little better than would have been the case if I had not established that I had a secretary.

When my darling mother-in-law Gladys Cooper was alive, we were once in Las Vegas together; I employed my gambit and had the clerk on the ropes and about to produce the accommodation. Suddenly Gladys spoke. 'You know perfectly well, Robert, you haven't reserved anything. You are only confusing the poor young man, and in any case I don't want to stay here. I am sure we shall be much happier in that nice motel next door.'

That would have been the end of that, except that the motel was full and we were obliged to crawl back ten minutes later.

'Another time perhaps you'll leave it to me,' I told her, surveying the inadequate accommodation with which I had eventually been provided.

'Another time,' replied Gladys, 'I will have *my* secretary handle the reservations. We stand a better chance with her; at least she exists!'

The reason why I am so well qualified to serve on the ROBERT Committee is that I have a nose for good restaurants. Put me down anywhere in a strange city and like a truffle hound straining at the leash, I will lead my party to the most delectable morsels. Where hotels are concerned, my perception is equally uncanny. Half a dozen steps across the threshold and I can tell whether a hotel is fully adjusted. If not, then I prefer to put my polo sticks back in the boot of the Rolls Royce and drive on. However imposing the façade, splendid the foyer, extravagant the furnishing, gorgeously costumed the bell-boys, luxurious the beds, unless a hotel is 'adjusted' neither you nor I are going to be happy there. In a restaurant one can return the boeuf Stroganoff to the chef with a courteous request that he should try again, and if he is prepared to do so, continue to toy with the caviare. The meal can still be salvaged. But there is nothing to be done with a hotel that is ill-adjusted, except pack and leave. It won't be difficult for you to do so early on your first morning, because the chambermaid will already have made an entrance, or at least knocked loudly on the door demanding to know if you rang. She does this to ensure that you will not oversleep and fail to give her a chance to do your room when it suits her to do so.

In all ill-adjusted hotel you will not be able to enjoy breakfast in bed. If you persevere with the telephone you will eventually be able to contact room service; but having done so you will be well advised to allow for the inevitable time lag and order luncheon. Last time I stayed at an hotel in New York I was amazed to find the breakfast trolley being trundled to my bedside a bare twenty minutes after I had put down the phone. 'This can't possibly be my breakfast,' I told the waiter. 'I ordered it under an hour ago.' The waiter shrugged his shoulders sympathetically and started to wheel the individually-gathered, sun-drenched blueberries with pasteurised double cream and thin (as you like them) hot cakes out of the door and back along the corridor. After a struggle I regained possession. 'Finders Keepers,' I told him.

The best room service in the world is enjoyed by guests of the Westminster Hotel, Paris Plage. Here one can reach out and press the bell push (suitably decorated with a picture of a waiter) and within two minutes the breakfast tray is resting lightly on one's stomach. The Westminster is, as I have noted, a supreme example of efficiency in this respect, but all over Europe, unlike the U.S.A., there are hotels which expect their guests to order breakfast around nine o'clock and are prepared to serve it within five minutes or so of their having done so. The secret is to have a kitchen on each floor; it is a secret which, except in rare instances, the Americans have not yet discovered; and for this reason, among others, it is not possible in my list of great hotels to include a single one in the United States. The absence of a bell push on the bedside table indicates that a hotel, despite its other pretensions, is understaffed.

For my money, and I admit a good deal of it is required whenever I am a guest there, the greatest hotel in the world is the Ritz in Paris. It is really two hotels, one situated in the Place Vendôme and the other in the Rue Cambon. I have never quite understood the geography of this beautiful building. To walk from the Place Vendôme to the Rue Cambon takes me at least five minutes and I have to cross several streets in order to do so, and yet if I make the same journey through the Ritz itself, along the elegant arcade with its show cases glittering with diamonds and broderie anglaise, I am there in half the time. A simple explanation may occur to the reader; one way one goes round, the other direct; but what happened to the streets? They certainly don't run through the Ritz itself, indeed in the centre of the hotel there are only a number of mysterious secret gardens, gravel-pathed and silent. I haven't the least idea how many bedrooms there are in the Ritz, only that in proportion to its size there are very few. It is the extravagance of the building which attracts me; I do not care for hotels which conserve space. I do not approve of batteries for hens or humans.

I am essentially a Rue Cambon man myself, although I often enter the hotel from the Place Vendôme, and admire the vast foyer, peopled at tea-time by archduchesses, elaborately bewigged and ex-monarchs waiting with well-bred boredom for their cucumber sandwiches. In the evening a small string orchestra plays in the restaurant, and an indescribable and reassuring melancholy hangs in the air. The diners have for the most part eaten all the caviare they are ever likely to actively enjoy on this earth, but the spoon still travels to the mouth loaded with the little black grains, and returns stained with carmine to the plate.

In the Espadron, which is the restaurant on my side of the hotel, the pace is altogether brisker. Caviare is eaten, but on toast. There is no vast entrance hall, and a comparatively narrow passage leads from the Rue Cambon up a short flight of steps to the reception desk; immediately opposite the hall porter's. Further on, where the passage ends and the glass doors of the Espadron open invitingly, is a small foyer usually cluttered with tables overflowing from the restaurant, and with French windows opening on to one of the gardens, where on summer evenings it is also possible to dine.

There is no better food, no more perfect setting for a meal in Paris except perhaps the Grand Vefour in the Palais Royal, with its ancient window engraved with an advertisement for Cherry Cobblers and its justly famous sommelier who refuses all invitations to try his hand at making one. You cannot, for that matter, get cherry cobblers in the Ritz, but you can get practically anything else and see practically everyone except le Président himself.

But it is with its bedrooms that the Ritz really scores. The timeless elegance of the furnishings, the gilt and the glitter, the huge ward-robes, the small sofas, the brass bedsteads – and the golden clocks, which I can never look at without a twinge of conscience; for once, long ago, I stopped all the clocks in the Ritz by yanking out a wire from one over my daughter's bed when she complained the tick was too loud and kept her awake. 'I'll soon stop that,' I told her, and I did. The trouble was that next morning no one would believe I was the culprit. In vain I telephoned the hall porter to confess my guilt.

'Impossible, Monsieur, you are not to blame,' he assured me. 'We are searching for the fault; it is the same in all the rooms; be patient.'

'At least,' I begged him, 'send someone up to my suite to investigate.'

'Useless, cher Monsieur,' he protested, 'the fault is with the elec-

160

tricity supply. Our engineers are in conference with the Minister.'

In the end I climbed on a chair and poked the wire back into its socket. At once my clock, like all the others in the Ritz that morning, started again. But, for me, the Ritz is the best hotel in the world not because of its electric clocks, or even despite them, but simply because it is the most comfortable to stay in. A guest in the Ritz is a guest of the Ritz, and no member of the staff ever forgets this simple fact for a single moment.

If you walk out of the Ritz into the Place Vendôme and turn left into the Rue de Rivoli you will come in a moment to a tea shop. Last summer, seated inside, I found an old friend and joined her for an éclair. It is sad how éclairs have almost entirely vanished from the tea table; in my youth they were obligatory, like conversation and visiting cards. In any case, my friend, a lady of enormous wealth, was lamenting the passing of the tea-cake.

'It is something I miss,' she remarked, 'like Baden Baden.'

'But surely,' I urged, 'Baden Baden remains.'

'Not for me,' she replied, 'and even if you were right, I don't suppose I should care for it nowadays. I used to go there when I was a little girl and what I remember most about Baden Baden were the Grand Dukes and their enormous trunks. The porters at Baden Baden railway station were the strongest porters in the world; they had to be. Nowadays,' my friend continued, 'one seldom sees a trunk as large as those, and when one does one has to be on one's guard. Last year I saw one at the Ritz, of all places. It was late at night and they were wheeling it along the passage. I happened to open my bedroom door and there it was. Behind walked the owner. I am certain he wasn't a Grand Duke. He looked,' she stabbed the air thoughtfully with her fork, 'as if he might have been a travelling salesman. One couldn't be sure, naturally. As you know, Robert dear, I am not a snob, moreover I am a very simple woman. I do not like cluttering up my life. I have entirely ceased to buy diamonds. I am no longer interested in property. I have a suite of rooms at the Ritz, another in the Hotel de Paris at Monte Carlo and a small house in London. With these, unlike most women I know, I am content, but if I am right about that traveller — and I hope very much I am not right — why then, I may have to consider reopening my apartment in Versailles, at any rate during the summer months; the danger, I imagine, would hardly arise in the winter; in any case at that time of the year I prefer Monte Carlo.'

'So do I,' I told her, and indeed I do. Summer and winter, come to that. I am drawn to Monte Carlo like a pilgrim to Mecca, or an art lover to Florence, because Monte Carlo still represents for me the centre of gambling in the world. In the centre of a whirlwind, although I have never proved this theory personally, there is said to be a vacuum. I *can* prove, however, that at the heart of Monte Carlo, in the great entrance hall of the Hotel de Paris, nothing stirs. You might argue that the real heart of Monte Carlo must be the casino, but the hotel is linked with it by a tunnel, so that it all really counts as one building. Here in the entrance hall, arranged possibly by some fabulous interior decorator, sit sometimes on sofas, sometimes on upright chairs, the Ladies and Gentlemen in Waiting. In enormous hats and wearing great quantities of jewellery and eye shadow, or blue-blazered and occasionally toupéed, they sit in the hotel as to the manor born. Elegant, resourceful, infinitely patient, they neither fidget nor fuss. Their purpose is to reassure the ordinary traveller that he too has arrived. Every now and then one of them will rise and make his or her way to the elevator, or out on to the terrace. It is not for us to enquire where they are going. They are going off duty, and that must suffice us.

The Hotel de Paris has more to offer even than its clientèle. It moves with the times and now has a superb roof restaurant and an indoor swimming pool. It also has the prettiest breakfast china in Europe and the unique advantage that people never stay here on business, or because they want to look at churches or trudge round picture galleries. They come some of them to gamble, all of them to put their feet up and to enjoy themselves. There are not nearly enough places where one can simply put one's feet up in Europe, but just on the edge of it, just before you cross the Bosphorous and find yourself in Asia, there stands at a small Turkish village called Yesilkov, twenty miles from Istanbul, on the sea of Marmora, my third great hotel, The Cinar.

There is something very attractive about the Sea of Marmora. I would not care to stay on the Bosphorous, which is surprisingly narrow, so that the Russian tankers finding their way up the channel occasionally lodge fast in some unfortunate Turk's front parlour. No such danger presents itself to guests of The Cinar, which passed all the tests to which I subjected it, and one that had not occurred to me — an earthquake. I am not fond of earthquakes, and this one caught me, as is their custom, unawares and about to step into a bath. I draped myself in a towel and hurried into the passage. A few doors opened and one or two guests made for the elevators, and others returned to their rooms as the tremors subsided. I hesitated, uncertain which course to pursue, and then happened to glance out of a window.

162

What I saw decided me to hurry down the staircase and rush pell mell into the garden, where I joined the dozen or so chefs whom I had spied from the corridor. Instinctively I felt these were the men to follow. They seemed content to stand around for a time chatting, and so was I. We were presently joined by an American professor who was, I had learned previously, in Turkey to arrange a program for a computer. It appeared that the American Government had given the Turkish Government a computer, for which naturally the latter were unable to find a use and to help them in their dilemma the Americans had now added a professor, whose task was to find a job worthy of the computer's prowess.

'I am thinking,' he told me, 'of putting it to work analysing the drinking water from various provinces. I don't know about the local authorities, but I am pretty sure the computer will get quite a shock.'

On the occasion of the earthquake I was delighted to see him. 'Has the danger passed?' I enquired. 'Is it safe for me to return and have my bath?' He consulted his watch and advised us all to wait another four minutes. We should either have another almost immediately, he insisted, or we shouldn't. I waited patiently while he continued to observe the minute hand. Eventually he looked up. 'Bath time,' he said reassuringly, and I and the chefs returned to our tasks.

While still in this part of the world, a word perhaps about the Hilton Hotel in Athens. Although not one for my list, it stands head and shoulders above all the other Hilton hotels at which I have stayed, including the London Hilton — which stands head and shoulders above Buckingham Palace. It would be foolish to belittle Mr. Hilton, or to deny that in many cities, such as Athens, he has imposed new standards of comfort and cleanliness not only on the natives but also on some of his guests. He reassures the American traveller — although not, oddly enough, the British. But then does *anything* reassure us? For myself it is the Hilton elevators which alarm. A slow mover, I am frequently attacked by the doors.

At the inaugural party to launch the London Hilton, I was retained to introduce the cabaret, which was performed between the courses and intended to emphasise the international flavour of the feast. Japanese jugglers following the birds' nest soup, a French singer the *poulet,* and so on. The waiter assigned to our table took a look round the affluent and distinguished guests, who included Mr. Paul Getty and Mr. Hilton himself. 'This looks,' he told us, 'as if it might turn out a funny evening. Ladies, will you please put your handbags in the centre of the table where we can all keep our eyes on them.' The American waiter is, of course, an expert on cutting the proceedings down to size. How often he demolishes the elegant, sophisticated atmosphere so carefully built up by host and proprietor by that honest shout of 'Who gets the consommé?' But his English cousin is seldom far behind. The best waiters, like the best lovers, are Latins. What the Englishman, the American, and for that matter the Australian, lack in technique both in bedroom and banqueting hall, they attempt unsuccessfully to cover up with bonhomie. Alas, there is more to laying a table or a lady than high spirits.

Outside of London, the traveller who stays in a British owned and operated hotel must not expect to be pampered. He will find meals are served when it suits the Hotel Catering Act to do so. Bedrooms are kept at a temperature which will encourage the client to spend money on gas or electric fires to stop shivering. Bathrooms are scarce, bleak and remote. What I find most depressing about British hotels is the display of literature in their public rooms. A British hotelier would rather shoot himself than buy a paper or a book for his guests to read. Such magazines as one finds in the smoking-room of The Crown, The Feathers or The George must not only be at least a year old and bereft of cover, but must also have been issued free, and deal with such subjects as canoeing or topiary. Anything, indeed, unlikely to excite or stimulate even the passing interest of an itinerant biscuit salesman.

The more modern the hotel in Britain the smaller the bedroom, the longer the corridor. The emphasis is on discipline. You are not, for instance, expected to upset your morning coffee. Having done so in Manchester one morning lately, I phoned for assistance. I was prepared for the staff to remove the sheets, but not the mattress. There was nothing for it but to get up — never a wise thing to do in Manchester until one is actually required at the theatre. I was stepping into the bath when the phone rang. Big Brother had been informed. 'We understand,' a voice told me, 'that you have soiled your bed. There will be an additional charge on your bill.' How different from the hotel in New Orleans, where after a stay of a fortnight there wasn't a bill at all. 'We like actors,' they told me, and charged only for telephone calls. Were it not that any hotel quite so recklessly conducted must have long since gone out of business, I would proudly include it in my list.

On the whole the British find little pleasure in staying in their own hotels, possibly because there is very little pleasure in doing so, with the exception of the top ten or so in London itself, and of course Claridges. No praise can ever be too high for this superb annexe to Buckingham Palace. It is the refuge of monarchs and presidents, protecting them while they reign and caring for them long after they have abdicated or been deposed. Uneasy lies the head which wears a crown, except on a Claridge's pillow slip. The management also entertain film producers, landed gentry, ambassadors, débutantes, actors intoxicated by their press cuttings and sober citizens. Immensely comfortable, superbly intimate, faultlessly maintained, more of a club than a hotel, and more of a home than either. The shining exception which proves the rule that the British don't understand the hotel business. Most surprising of all, there are few foreigners on its staff.

Oddly enough there was a British waiter on the staff of my fifth great hotel, the Imperial, Vienna, when I stayed there shortly after it had reopened. Vienna is a city of make-believe. Where else would you find the horn of a unicorn on display next to a golden rose? It is a city where horses prance under the chandeliers in the riding school and where the Russians, taking a hint from their hosts, stabled their own cavalry in the ballroom of the Imperial Hotel and roasted an ox on its marble staircase. But when they left, their hosts, no whit abashed by such vandalism, managed to get everything back in place along with the gilt mirrors and the chandeliers, and opened for business within a year.

Very comfortable it was when I was there making a film with Yul Brynner and Deborah Kerr, and first fell in love with Anne Jackson. Yul's part in the picture demanded he should be constantly chewing on a wine glass, but the rest of us sat around happily in the hotel dining room, munching Rhine salmon and wild strawberries, and occasionally venturing forth to the location, accompanied by a vast quantity of cardboard on which cotton wool had been affixed and which had to be scattered over the countryside to represent the snows of yesteryear in which we had optimistically commenced the shooting, and which had long since melted away.

Presently I was joined by my wife and children who in those days were fascinated by the enormous gas balloons sold in the Prater just beside the Great Wheel immortalised in *The Third Man*. These they would bear home in triumph and then, forgetful as ever, release, whereupon the balloons would sail upwards and bump along the ceiling. As long as the children stayed with me it seemed as if in our sitting-room there was always a porter perched on a stepladder.

'You really mustn't bother him again,' I would tell my son.

'But he likes it, Pa, he really does,' would be the reply. Not of course the only reason for including the Imperial, but certainly one of them.

165

A hotel is only as good as its staff, and my sixth among the giants, although it possesses an exceptional one, will persist in the supreme folly of dressing it up as if for a children's fancy dress party. Let not the traveller be dismayed, therefore, when on arrival, the door of his car is opened by a gentleman sweltering in the guise of a Beefeater, or when his luggage is unloaded by another dressed as if for the paddy fields. He is not in the Tower of London or Vietnam, he is not even in Disneyland, he has merely arrived at the Century Plaza in Beverly Hills, California. There are various theories about the costumes. The hotel is built on part of what used to be the Twentieth Century Lot and some think the film company threw in the wardrobe along with the land. Others see a sinister attempt to lull the nation into a false sense of security so that when the threatened Chinese invasion finally takes place, the American citizens will be caught unawares. 'Don't worry,' they will be telling each other, 'they are merely bell-hops from the Century Plaza.'

Once you have winced over the threshold, however, you will be very comfortable indeed in this hotel. It has the most efficient elevators, the best room service and the most comfortable beds of any hotel in America. It is beautifully quiet and, except for the dressing up already noted, quietly beautiful.

Not as beautiful, of course, as my last great hotel, the Gritti Palace of Venice, but then the latter has the manifestly unfair advantage of the Grand Canal. No other hotel in the world can compete with such a setting, and one can pay no higher tribute to the Gritti than to note that it deserves to be exactly where it is. It has the incomparable advantage of not having been built as a hotel. It was originally intended to be, and indeed still is, a Palace. The corridors meander, the bathrooms are never quite where you expect, the furniture not dreamt up by an interior decorator, but collected piece by piece over the years, until at last the room is complete and fit for a guest. Last time I stayed, I sent a bedside lamp crashing onto the marble floor. 'If I can afford to pay for it, I will,' I told the desk. They dismissed the suggestion with a chuckle. Venice is a long way from Manchester.

There are other hotels I have stayed in and been comfortable and content: the Mandarin in Hong Kong, the Tokyo Hilton, the Pierre Marqueez in Acapulco, the Black Buck in Wiesbaden, and, surprisingly, the Europa in Leningrad, but the seven I have written of are the tops. They have a reputation for perfection which over the years they have cherished and striven successfully to maintain. Most of us go through life haunted by a few anonymous, pleasurable scents. A flower sniffed in childhood, a special kind of wood fire, hops drying, a horse being shod, furniture polish, vanilla, honeysuckle, straight bourbon. Now and again, perhaps in a strange house, or walking in the country, or passing along some city street, there comes borne over the air towards us a remembered fragrance, which delights. Thus, when I first cross the lobby of a new hotel I will pause for a moment with my nostrils hopefully flared. What is the scent for which I am patiently sniffing the air? It is the smell of confidence which comes from perfection.

Insecuricor

Nothing makes me feel less secure than Securicor itself. Sometimes on the motorways we pull up next to these grey, grim armoured vehicles in which the banks reportedly move bullion from branch to branch; one inspects the po-faced gentlemen behind the wire netting and they inspect us, with their trained expression of hostile, wary contempt, and I marvel that they should be allowed not only on the roads, but in the country, and fall to wondering how, given half a chance, I would burst in and, seizing their clubs, remove their helmets and after a few sharp blows, leave them, not for the first time, trussed and bound in the back of their own vans while I speed away, the booty in my boot.

Half the world, and I have no doubt the other half as well, but I have not yet been to it, is spoiled for me by the private armies of the security organizations which infest the beaches of Africa and the linen shops of Fifth Avenue. I don't want to be guarded as I lie toasting under an umbrella on a Mombassa beach, clad only in my bathing dress. What could I possibly be wearing that anybody else could want? Yet up and down and round me are steel-helmeted and gaitered (against snakes? Are there snakes on the sand, and if so, why wasn't I told?) Securicor patrols. Each time he passes, he tucks his baton under his arm, halts briefly and raises his hand in some crazy, quasi-military salute. Why? What is the purpose of this foolery? Are we expecting a tribe of cannibals? Are the Masai on the march? Or some sneak thief, bent double, flitting from coral rock to coral rock, collecting cameras, sunglasses, half-opened bottles of Ambre Solaire? Outside, inside the jewellers' shops, the banks, the hotel lobbies, circle the vultures, reminding visitor and citizen alike that nothing is secure until they have secured it. What nonsense, what rubbish this great protection racket has become. How foolish of Government and citizens alike to allow it, and how fatally divisive the device, foreverlastingly reminding the haves that the have nots are ready to snatch, challenging the criminals, encouraging the tearaways. 'Here it is,' they tell them, 'come and get it if you can.'

A policeman should, and often does, reassure. He is there to see fair play, to tell us the time, to point in the direction of the Post Office, to take our side against the criminal. But the private cop has no such allegiance to the public and is suspicious of any enquiry. He is there to protect the booty, no matter how it was obtained. He is there to see that the rich grow richer and the poor keep their distance, and if they don't know what their distance is, he is ready to give them a shove back behind the ropes.

It started with the Corps of Commissionaires. If your daughter was being married, you hired one to keep an eye on the presents and help park the cars. Later some of the more expensive shops hired them to ameliorate the feelings of their overcharged customers. In America between the wars they elaborated the notion. They armed private cops with guns and let them patrol motion picture lots to keep the actors from escaping. I don't think they ever shot one; in those days we were too valuable.

In New York recently I was horrified by the hysteria. As dusk fell, the hotel lobbies filled up not with the café society fun lovers of yesterday, or the out-of-towners intent on an evening of hell raising, but with security guards. Main entrances were closed, swing doors secured, entrance effected through side passages and up emergency staircases.

Even the New York taxi cabs have been refashioned into armoured cars; steel bulwarks protect the drivers from such desperate characters as myself. Payment is made through a slit in the armoured glass. What rubbish, what nonsense, what poltroonery! A friend, driving from the airport recently at two o'clock in the morning, found the driver had not only secured himself but his passenger, locking the doors of the cab by remote control before switching off the taxi meter. This is kidnap, my friend told himself, and was astonished to arrive safely at his destination. His relief was almost as great as the fare demanded and gratefully paid.

No wonder the New York theatres are empty, the restaurants deserted, the night clubs closed. Let us beware lest London follows this pattern of defeat. We are not all extras in a new horror film. There is no King Kong loose in our cities, we do not have to rush hither and thither in senseless panic to heighten the dramatic effect and satisfy the director. We are the many perfectly able to protect ourselves against the few; if we need more policemen we can afford to hire them ourselves. What we cannot afford is big business trying to persuade us that they can take over law and order if we are prepared to pay extra for the service. If we don't stop the rot now, the next body of men to demand protection at their hands will be the Police Force.

I warn the Home Secretary that when the first security guard shows up on Bognor beach, I shall emigrate.

Eating Up

'Eat up, Master Robert,' nurse would urge, 'show me a nice clean plate. If you can't manage that last piece it means you don't want pudding.' It meant nothing of the kind. I always looked forward to pudding, still do. Eating habits formed at the nursery table are irreversible. An overweight child grew into an overweight adult. It's true that there was a school of nursery thought which encouraged me occasionally to leave something for manners, but this referred to the last piece of bread and butter before it had been actually transferred to my plate. Once that happened it was my duty to gobble it up. Even mustard was not lightly set aside. Mrs. Colman was apparently gowned on the proceeds of mustard waste. My mother enjoyed repeating a story about a maid reproved for not washing the dishes properly. 'The mustard, Ma'am, was there before I came.' My enjoyment of food was constantly being interrupted by bilious attacks which necessitated my lying fully dressed on the sofa, eyes closed, a water biscuit within reach, alongside a small basin.

I was not a child who shone on the sports field. There are no pictures of me cross-legged, squatting at the feet of the Cricket Captain, supporting the shield which I had assisted the team to win, but there is a fading sepia print of myself at the age of eight, presiding at a feast at Geronimo's, looking in my Eton collar and with my hair carefully quiffed, like a young Al Capone. Geronimo's of Folkestone was a restaurant of renown, famed for meringues, a dish of which I have always been a connoisseur. Meringues Chantilly, and not of course the vulgar Meringues Glacés. At schools I complained bitterly of the fare, at the age of nine protesting to the Headmaster of the establishment at which I was spending a term — I seldom stayed longer at any school — about his serving me up fried bread and jam and maintaining it was a pudding. The argument ended, as arguments are wont with schoolmasters, in blows, but not before it had

171

produced my first aphorism. 'There is a time,' I told the entire school, 'when catering ceases to be catering and becomes rationing.'

I repeated the remark not so long ago at Ayres Rock, finding myself hungry in the great open wasteland of Central Australia after the table d'hôte lunch. Dinner that same evening, and after my protest, was more plentiful, but I remain unconvinced that food in the Outback is not cooked and served up by chefs specially imported from English boarding schools. Travellers in Australia should at all costs avoid the counter lunch offered in public houses, but in most towns and certainly in all cities there are delicious meals to be found for the trouble of looking for them. In Lorne on the Victorian coast and not far from the celebrated Geelong Grammer School, there is a marine café which serves the best crayfish I have ever eaten. In Freemantle there is the Oysterbed Restaurant, in Adelaide The Barn, in Melbourne Fanny's and in Sydney Mon Coeur, all superb; even their specialities can be safely recommended, although I am always somewhat chary of such taste sensations, and make it a rule to eschew dishes which the chef must have been asked to prepare time and time again.

Nowhere does the national character assert itself more stridently than at the dining table. The French, who conceived the idea of cooking for gain and opened the first restaurant in the Palais Royal once it had been vacated by the aristocrats, have now lost heart. They have had it too good, too many tourists have professed themselves satisfied with the tarte de la maison, the lack of fresh vegetables and the endless monotony of the sauce Béchamel now go unchallenged. Only the bread is what it was. Here in England we meet our children fresh out of school, but at noon the French parent has a rendezvous at the baker's.

In Spain service continues late into the night; the rich eat too much, the poor not enough. In Germany everybody eats too much. Italians eat extravagantly, Greeks cautiously, Americans at speed. They seldom linger longer than is necessary. In elegantly contrived Beverly Hills bistros, baroque Chicago Pump Rooms, Fifth Avenue Regency parlours or exotic San Francisco fish tanks, nothing ever stops the hired help destroying the ambiance with 'Who gets the check?'

But what of the British? Where do we stand, or rather, sit? Well, at least we have learnt that no visitor in his senses would ever eat the sort of food we dish out to ourselves. They will never, unless they are very unlucky indeed, have to eat in our railway stations, in our prisons, in our hospitals, in our schools or on our racecourses. We know better than to advertise English cooking. Our restaurants and hotels are staffed by foreigners. In London, and indeed throughout the whole of the British Isles, you will find the French cook better than they do in France, Turkish chefs exert themselves more in London than in Istanbul, and the best Chinese food in the world is prepared in Cheltenham.

When you have had enough of our towers and palaces, our cathedrals and castle ruins, you will find the bistro in the keep, the take-away curry shop in the pantiles and the wine bar (Spanish type) triumphant where once stood ye boring olde English Tea Shoppe.

Trouble at the George & Dragon

Asked where I live, I am always most happy to tell people and usually volunteer the information that I have lived there for thirty-odd years. I come of a generation who found virtue in longevity, who feel that a long and happy marriage is something to boast of, who derive smug satisfaction from staying afloat. We called our house Fairmans and it's a great convenience having a short address. I cannot abide men who print their business address with a sequence of numbers. Choose one, I would say to them, don't show off. But of course I show off nearly all the time. Fairmans, Wargrave, I tell shop assistants, not even adding Berks, which might be more prudent: there are, alas, other Wargraves. It can matter to few that over the years I have put down my roots, but it matters to me, which is why I got so cross the other evening at the George and Dragon.

Turning out of the gate of Fairmans, you can either go left or right. Left takes you up past Pennies Lane, once the main road, and now signposted 'unsuitable for motor traffic', but which unaccountably occasionally sprouts abandoned vehicles and car seats. Pennies Lane leads, if you are a stout walker, back down into Wargrave; it is deeply muddy and overgrown, a hazard for the very young, and rapidly becoming the same for me. More often the grandchildren and I continue along the macadam to the village of Crazies Hill and the Horns public house, an excellent pull up for chips, Coca-Cola and a small vodka tonic. Refreshment downed, we normally turn round and walk back: it is not quite far enough away to telephone to demand a rescue party. On the way home we detour to Rebecca's Well to fill our medicine bottle with magic water and wish. This is a genuine magic well, the home of a vast number of magic toads, and if on arrival home, having made the wish, we deposit the medicine bottle in a safe place and wait twenty-four hours, the water will turn pink, supposing our wish to be in the process of being granted.

174

The only other possible excitement in the village of not very attractive-looking cottages and a church hall of almost ostentatious piety, is The Crazies itself, a neo-Georgian town hall which once graced Henley and was removed lock, stock and parlour to its present site. Why and when exactly, I have never enquired. I am not a curious man. For a long time my younger son tried to convince me that Hitler lived in the village, and claimed to have seen him on several occasions. However, I never took the matter one step further. If Hitler did indeed settle here after he escaped the bunker, he is now dead. Now and again, give and take twice in the summer, I pass the Horns and with the unmistakeable pious expression of those on the highway who are not cadging a lift but going for a walk, march down through the gambling gap, a lane which gets its name from the fact that it is single-tracked and much favoured by fast sports cars, and on along the river bank to Hurley. I admire the canoeists and the assorted company on the motor boats and when I have got my breath back and two large vodkas and tonics inside me, ring home and invite any member of the family who answers to join me in the bar, bringing cash and a motor.

Turning right out of the home gate, once you have manoeuvred the corner and passed the farms which lie on either side of the road, there is nothing for a long, straight mile. There is not much to amuse children, they can walk for a time in the ditch and get very wet and they can lie down and grizzle. There are one or two gates to climb, and lorries to count as they tear by. There is the occasional horse and rider and the occasional dog; there is even nowadays a guard dog, or so it would seem, in a fenced enclosure at the very end of the road where a captain of industry has recently tied up. How then do I persuade the young or myself to turn right and walk the whole, incredibly boring mile and a half to Wargrave itself? Well, the answer quite simply is, or was until the other evening, the George and Dragon.

The inn, which stands on the river bank, has since I can remember been a tied house, and up to a year ago had a pleasing river frontage with a sort of wintergarden into which, after they had tied up their boats at the landing stage, the weekend yachting crowd would tumble to get out of the rain and their oilskins. We never actually had a visit from Heath himself, but lived in hope. Now that they've rebuilt the place and upped the prices, the ambiance has departed and the George and Dragon looks like any other modern roadhouse, furnished with that customary lack of taste which gives to modern saloon lounges the impression that the Garnetts have at last been able

175

to spread themselves a bit. The attraction, as far as my family was concerned, was that the last quarter mile of our journey was downhill, and we could sit in the sun lounge, as it was optimistically called, and see a bit of life while nibbling chips and sucking happily through our straws and waiting for the rescue craft. There has never been any question of walking home uphill from Wargrave, much too far we are all agreed.

Above the sun lounge were bedrooms with balconies. Various aunts and uncles, and indeed my mother, have in their time bedded down there and been most comfortable. But last week my proprietorial interest in the establishment was rudely challenged. They didn't want to take my cheque. Not for Cokes and chips, but for a rather large bill for five and, I must be fair, a rather good dinner.

'I live here,' I told the head waiter, who seemed to have as much difficulty understanding my rough Berkshire dialect as I did his suave Continental undertone.

'I would like only your car number,' he seemed to be saying.

'What car number? I came in a friend's car. I don't know the number. Come to that, I don't know my own number. I do know my name is *Robert Morley*.' It had, I must confess, no magic for him. 'You must have seen me on the late show, the chat show, the — don't you,' I ended weakly, 'ever go to *the theatre*?'

The fellow was not to be deflected by idle chatter. 'We have a rule,' he told me, 'I dare not break it.'

'This is absurd,' I attacked from a new direction, 'I have just come back from Kenya. Everyone took my cheque in Kenya, even the game.' I suppose the second bottle of Burgundy was a mistake; it's no good getting facetious with foreigners. 'Send for the brewer,' I told him, 'ring up Courage himself and explain the dilemma.' I seem to remember I met a Courage once. 'Mr. Courage knows me well.' On such insubstantial ground do we build when excited. 'Tell Mr. Courage I am proposing to pay by cheque.' The headwaiter moved to the telephone, but only to summon the hotel manager. To my surprise she turned out not only to be British, but I judged about sixteen. She came fresh on the scene with the self possession of one accustomed to being obeyed.

'We have a rule here,' she told me, 'and we stick by it. We do not accept cheques without a banker's reference. I am sorry, but I cannot change the rule, even if I wished to do so.'

'I am a resident,' I told her, 'I live up the road. I have lived up the road before you were born.'

'Residents,' she told me, with appalling but disarming frankness, 'often give more trouble than visitors.'

'Which accounts no doubt,' I told her, 'for the reason we are your sole guests this evening. You have frightened the simple villagers away, demanding cash, questioning their bank balances, their credit ratings.'

In the end she decided to bend the rules if I for my part would write my address on the back of the cheque. I refused. I can't remember why, something I suppose to do with feeling affronted. Nowadays I don't affront easily. The time when I would stand shaking at the bank counter while the clerk went to verify my balance, is past. He may still go to verify my balance, but I no longer shake; there's always an overdraft to be obtained. At the present rate of interest, they'd be mad not to encourage the customer to overdraw.

But what of the George and Dragon, the absentee landlord, the endless petty harrassment of the customers who make life possible and profitable for the vast conglomerates of big business who lord it over them? Let them stop issuing edicts to employees about collecting the cash because they are too occupied forming cartels and destroying competition to give the customers what is their right, the benefit of the doubt. A man in this country is assumed to be innocent until he has been proved guilty; assumed to be solvent until proved otherwise. If he chooses to pay by cheque he is entitled to do so; the brewers are not entitled to question his credit. They display no notices demanding cash or money in advance. We, the consumers, have a right to withhold our credit cards, to refuse our addresses. Once we have eaten the food and drunk the wine, the hotelier must trade on our terms or not at all.

In future I propose to arm myself with a peacock's feather and place it on the table beside me when I call for the bill. If my credit is questioned, I shall employ it in the Roman manner and simply sick up.

THE
SOUND
OF
MORLEY

Confessions of a Pudding Man

I am a pudding man. Nothing depresses me more than a meal which doesn't finish with one. 'Just coffee for me, thanks,' is not a phrase in my book. However boring the occasion, I perk up when they wheel in the sweet trolley. I inspect it as I would a guard of honour, I insist the jellies should be standing to attention, the rhubarb, although I never touch it, pale pink, the chocolate sauce dark and mysterious. I cannot contemplate a spoilt trifle. 'What was in that?' I ask, as I wave away the half-filled dish and wait for the replacement. Sometimes there are several trolleys going the rounds. It is as well to inspect them all. They are seldom identical. The first lesson I taught my children was never to show your hand when being served from a trolley. Never ask for a little of that and a little of that, please. If you have decided on profiteroles and syllabub, encourage the waiter to pile your plate with the former, and only when he has put back the spoon, suddenly, and on the spur of the fork, as it were, demand the syllabub.

Because I am a great artist myself, I know the disappointment of rejection. I know what it is like to 'bang on the slap' and find the house empty. I know what it must be like for a chef to send out a Crème Honoré and have it returned untouched. When no one bought his paintings, Gauguin, or was it Van Gogh, cut off his own ear. A kitchen is full of knives. I must put no similar temptation in the way of a pastrycook.

I look forward to the petit fours, often nibbling the spun sugar in the swan's beak, or breaking off a piece of the basket and chewing the wicker work. I am not fond of marzipan. It is not a medium in which a chef does his finest work. The best sweet trolleys are always to be found in Italian restaurants, the most meagre in Indian ones. The two finest puddings I have ever tasted are the circular mille feuilles obtainable at the Château de Madrid and an Orange Boodle

Fool my daughter occasionally makes at the weekends when we have company.

I am a lifelong enemy of tapioca, but every now and then am seduced by a prune. I am still fond of a good meringue, but never hope to taste again quite the perfection of my grandmother's. I was smaller in those days, but a meringue should always be judged, like a vegetable marrow, by its size.

Of my schooldays I remember with pleasure only the tuck shop on the days I could afford a tenpenny mess (one banana, two scoops ice-cream and extra cream). I don't say I was happy then, but I was a little less miserable. While others dreamt of success on the playing fields, my private fantasy was a box of milk flake bars to myself.

For a time after I left school I was hooked on Walnut Whips, but ever afterwards have been a milk chocolate addict. I share my craving with one of my cats. Together we prowl the house, searching for the cache where my wife has hidden the bars she buys for the children. When we discover the hoard, we demolish it. Naturally, my share is larger than Tom's, but once we have awoken our taste buds, nothing can stop us. I have even known Tom to eat the silver paper. I have left many things unfinished in my life, but never a bar of chocolate. I haven't a wisdom-tooth in my head, but thank the Lord I still have a sweet one.

Hell is . . .

Hell is a play by Brecht, Hamlet acted by Nicol Williamson, a word from Lord Soper. Hell is a medical examination for an insurance policy, a shop like Harrods. Hell was always macaroni cheese, and lately the Earls Court Road. Hell is a story I've told too often and a letter from my accountant before I've opened it. Hell is a letter from my accountant after I've opened it. Hell is knowing how much I have in the bank. Hell is the bathroom scales and the unexplained blemish on the end of my nose. Hell was my name on a games list at school, and a lout who terrorised me when I rode my tricycle.

I know my Hell can't be the right one. Good heavens, there are people who are prepared to pay to see Nicol Williamson, sane, ordinary, well-informed folk who probably shop at Harrods on the way to the theatre. It is patently absurd to worry about health or money. I don't really worry about my weight. I certainly don't want to know about it, any more than I want to know about Hell.

I shall feel a perfect fool if I open my eyes after I've died, and find things exactly as predicted by the devout, by the Seventh Day Adventists, Jehovah Witnesses, or Aimée Semple Macpherson, who once explained the whole thing to me seated on a motorcycle and dressed as God's Cop, or so she claimed. Could she have been right? Could they all have been right? Is there a final reckoning, and if so, how shall I fare?

'But we told you,' they will insist, 'we kept on telling you. Why on earth didn't you believe us? It was perfectly obvious, surely? You weren't just there to enjoy yourself. You were supposed to be preparing for the life eternal.'

'But what happens?' I shall ask piteously. 'What happens now?'

'What do you expect will happen? You flunked, you're for it, old man.'

But who will be there with me? None of my aunts, that's for sure.

They all believed in the life eternal, and they were right. I always contradicted them, and I was wrong. Not all of them, of course, would have expected me to go to Hell. Some of them might even have been mildly surprised, especially my aunt Evelyn, my champion aunt, who bought three vacuum cleaners from me my first morning in the trade. She surely must be in Heaven by now, that is of course always supposing there is a heaven, which I don't. It's not that I cannot visualise myself in a state of permanent preservation, even in a position of perpetual worship. I am confident that I am the sort of person God would like to have around, but on my journey through life, if indeed it is possible to travel in the recumbent position I have so frequently and for such long periods adopted, I have met so few who seem qualified to accompany me to Paradise. There simply aren't sufficient of the right people to fill the place and if the Almighty doesn't want Heaven to look like Lord's Cricket Ground on the final day of The Test, He will be well advised to cancel the match. Most people are so much more boring than I am. Very few of them have the quality of being able to amuse the Almighty, indeed I can count on the fingers of one hand (I have four) the men and women I have met whom God and I would welcome as they stepped through the pearly gates — Bernard Shaw, Sybil Thorndike, Wilfrid Hyde White and although I am not absolutely certain about him, Marty Feldman. A personal choice, you may argue, and one that does not include members of my own family, but then naturally we shall enter in a body. Nevertheless, even at this rate the place can hardly be said to be filling up, and though I imagine there may have been a few early arrivals, such as Michaelangelo, Shakespeare and just conceivably Moses, it is unlikely, in my opinion at any rate, that the party would ever really get off the floor.

At school Divinity was my best subject.It usually is with backward pupils. But I have never had much subsequent joy from the Bible. I don't really care for the style, but I have always been very fond of the Parable of the Vineyard. It has always seemed eminently fair to me that workers who arrive late on the scene should not be penalised. I arrived very late on my scene. Indeed I was thirty before my weekly wage reached double figures, and I was usually the last one to be hired in the casting office. I am not a man who has read widely, preferring to keep my mind relatively uncluttered with the ideas of others, so that any of my own thoughts may have room to manoeuvre. Unless you have a first-class mind it is a great mistake to afford it a first-class education. It is daunting to discover that everything has already been said and thought. My ideas may not shatter, but I am always pleasurably surprised to have conceived them, and cannot help being struck with their originality and brilliance. Better and especially classically educated men are, on the other hand, often bored when I expound them. 'Plato said that,' they tell me. 'Did he, indeed?' I take care never to read Plato, but it would be an overstatement to maintain that I have taken care not to read the Bible. The idea has simply never occurred to me, and therefore I do not know whether there is in the Good Book a reliable description of Hell, or for that matter Heaven, though I seem to remember both subjects were touched on in Revelations, but it is too late now for me to bother.

If I believe anything about a God, it is that He is a God anxious for me not to worry my head about life after death, or for that matter death after life. I never expect to meet Him, and I cannot go along with those who believe in a sort of instant judgement. It would take far too long to decide most people's cases (not mine, perhaps, but most people's) for considered judgement to be practicable, let alone just. I don't know why I should expect judgement to be just, but I suppose that comes of being British. Italians, for instance, may find it easier to believe, but I am not Italian, and I would certainly be the last to wish Heaven to be filled with them. They are a gifted race, and in the kitchen at any rate, superior to ourselves, but cooking in Heaven is not seriously envisaged by the faithful, although I suppose it's more than possible it might take place in Hell, in which case it would surely be the sort of cooking I watched on television the other evening, where the butter was shaped like a rose, and dusted with edible gold dust. Is Fanny Craddock really the Devil in disguise? 'Why on earth should she be?' you ask, and alas, I cannot answer, except to postulate that anyone could be the Devil, or anyone could go to Heaven or to Hell for that matter, and I should not be a penny the wiser. All I can affirm is that Hell for me is butter shaped like a rose and dusted with edible gold dust.

The Spirits of Christmas Past

I am always delighted to see the Three Wise Men, they keep themselves so fit. I can't remember how long ago I bought them, or where, but each year I wander from room to room, holding them in my hand and looking for fresh terrain on which to stand them. In the end they always take their accustomed place above the window in the hall. There's a ledge which suits them perfectly, each walking a pace behind the other in the general direction of the golden star, with which I am not so pleased. It becomes increasingly difficult to disguise the tarnish. I am a clumsy man, not wont, or, indeed, able usually to let my fingers do the walking, but the decorations are my special province. If I was honest I would say what I look forward to most each Christmas is the brandy butter and getting my two hundredth Christmas card. I need two hundred to fix to the beams in the living-room. Without them the room is hopeless. I have tried alternative decorations and failed.

In point of fact I have tried alternative decorations almost everywhere, but each year repeat the pattern with only one or two minor alterations. The bandsmen from Tokyo can stand on the mantelpiece and the Holy Family take their places on the window ledge, or vice versa. There are some dilapidated musical instruments which pin either up the stair rail or around the grandfather clock. I am sick to death of three cardboard angels with feather skirts. Each year they come out of their box and almost at once retire back into it. It is not just that they are common — they are not, for instance, as common as the Hong Kong plastic mines, or even the Christmas Tree Fairy herself — it's just that I hate them as much as I love the owls, the beautiful white owls who perch in the holly branches, and the golden mobile, the pièce de résistance on the top landing, which only my boundless courage and total disregard of personal danger enables me to fix each Christmas Eve, balancing on the topmost of the folding steps.

186

I buy my new decorations each August in a shop which sells to the trade. Go in September and it's all over. In September they sell Easter bunnies. I like that very much. I admire people who plan ahead. I revere those who put things behind them. Myself, I job back. I want this Christmas to be as much like the last as possible. I hold on as a man catapulted into the water will hold on to an upturned keel, surprised at first how easily it helps him to stay afloat, feeling as yet no numbness in his finger-tips.

Talking of finger-tips, I must try not to be the first this year to pull the cracker, to put on the cap, to read the riddle, to hog the enjoyment. I have had over sixty Christmases and enjoyed them all, except possibly my first, and for all I know I may have enjoyed that one too. On my sixth they gave me the Delhi Durbar. I don't remember what I was given last year or the year before or the year before that. The only Christmas present I ever remember was the Delhi Durbar. It came complete with the King Emperor and his Queen, the elephants and the ceremonial pavilion. It came in a flat red box, the sort of box jigsaws came in, but this was no puzzle. It was what I wanted most in the whole world, it was all I wanted. It was perfection, and I have never, never forgotten the box on the drawing-room floor under the Christmas tree at six o'clock on Christmas Eve. It was not done up in idiotic wrapping paper, it was not tied with string. All I had to do was to lift off the lid and start taking the sepoys and the gurkhas, the horses and the tigers out one by one and stand them on the carpet.

So why go on, you ask, why if six was perfect try for sixty-six, why not forget the whole thing this year? Take oneself off to the splendid quiet of an Imperial Hotel at some neglected, out-of-season watering place, and hole up with an electric blanket on the bed and a 'Do not Disturb' sign on the door handle. I have thought of it. I have made a few discreet enquiries. 'Are you full at Christmas, and what are your rates?' To do it properly I suppose I would have to come down to Christmas Dinner and eat my way solemnly through to the mince pies, eyeing the solitary cracker on the table, staring out front, intensely proud, utterly alone — the sort of part Aubrey Smith (or I, for that matter) would have given our eye-teeth for. But no, I have to be home to open the cards, and before anyone else has a chance to read them, impale them with a drawing-pin up aloft. Long, short, long, short is the pattern. The picture families I do save for the mantelpiece. There are only a few of those, alas — the Yehudi Menuhins whom I hardly know, and the David Tomlinsons whom I know very well, my niece's family and sometimes the odd godchild or a celebrated photographer out on a spree. I have never had one from the Queen, but then of course she has never had one from me. I do get one from the Gaekwar of Baroda, but it is almost severely simple and although I sometimes save it for some guest to open up and read His Highness's message, they seldom seem to bother. There was a theatrical manager who used to imagine himself still an officer and gentleman and always sent pictures of regimental carnage, but these I neither pinned nor planted. They were not, I told myself, the real spirit of Christmas, and I laid them on one side to be used only in dire emergency.

For years the village in which I live used to support a company of bell-ringers, and on the appointed evening they would arrive and march into the living-room, where we had only just switched off the telly and were hoping they wouldn't notice the fumes. They put their bells on a small portable card table and kept picking them up and putting them down again with a sort of sustained patience, and if you listened very carefully and had an ear for music, it was possible to discover some sort of tune. Then came the moment for which I was waiting, when the head man would enquire whether we had a favourite carol. It was the signal that the performance was about to finish; it was the equivalent of the 'and now one final question' on the chat show. Loudly I would call for Good King Wenceslas. 'Again?' they were wont to enquire. 'Again,' I would tell them. 'I can't hear it often enough,' I would lie. Then cakes and ale and five pounds in the hat, or possibly a bit less, and God rested the Merry Gentlemen for another year. Now we have carol singers; they don't come in, but I feel just as much of a fool standing in the garden pretending I like being sung at. I would as lief have a Hungarian violinist bending over my crêpes suzette in some ghastly foreign bistro.

So what's it all about, then, you ask, and I can honestly tell you I don't know. Have they spoilt Christmas, and if so, who are they? The butchers, the bakers, the candlestickmakers? The poor we cannot forgive or the homeless we will not house or the hungry we have not fed or the prisoners we have not set free? Are they the ones who announce in the agony columns that they are not sending cards this year, but have made a donation to the Lifeboat Fund, or are they people like you and me, who always want the sort of Christmas we had last year or the year before that, or sixty years ago, who want to stand on the other side of the drawing-room door and still be able to reach up and open it when the clock strikes and find the Delhi Durbar under the tree?

Myself and I

What pride we fatties take in shedding a few pounds; how we love to be able to button our coats once more and enquire of our friends whether they have noticed anything about us. 'Lost a bit, haven't you?' 'Yes,' we tell them, adding as reassurance that this is not a wasting disease, but sheer will power. My present pathetic attempt to join the ranks of the sightly was triggered off by a paperback I picked up in Deauville after a particularly unsuccessful evening at the tables.

The morning after is for me a time of resolution. I wake early and lie in bed cursing my folly. I am not a good loser. I read once that all gamblers are ugly, and on such mornings I recall the faces around the table and compare my own in the mirror of the hotel bedroom. 'So that's why I gamble,' I tell myself, 'because I am not beautiful.' From now on, I decide, everything will be different. No more lunatic forays to the green baize. But good resolution does not end there. My whole way of life must in future be purposeful and to begin with I must change my image. Remorse and diet complement each other. Having shed the weight I can begin to search afresh for the treasure which lies just beneath the surface of my mind. I will write a play, or better still a novel, and sell the film rights for a fortune. It would be simpler and quicker probably to win the money on the football pools, but that way lies not redemption. Banning myself from casinos and racetracks I vow never again to fill in a football coupon. It doesn't last, naturally, but while it does I am proud of the fact that I am no longer myself. I pass up the rolls and butter, disdainfully regard the plates of others, and when the call for luncheon comes, sit on at my desk, admiring the waistline which is to come. One meal a day is enough for anyone, even a dog.

My paperback tells me that there is scarcely a man or woman in America or western Europe who isn't, like myself, overweight. We are all, it seems, dying of over-eating. The world is no longer divided between the fat and the thin, but between the very fat and the fairly fat. Why this theory should help keep me on a diet I don't know, but it does — at the moment. I shall soon be back, I suppose, to the old sweet trolley, the spinning ball, toast and butter and baccarat, but meanwhile I don't plan to join Gamblers' Anonymous or the Weight-watchers. I don't want to belong to a group. It's just possible that there are people as silly as I, or even sillier, but I don't particularly want to know them. Above all I don't want to know myself. Not because I don't love myself, I do, passionately, but because I am fascinated by my unpredictability. What, I wonder, am I going to think next, let alone do? All the years I have known myself still leave me totally unprepared for my next thought or action. There are patterns, of course, of a sort. I know, for instance, that so many times a day I shall stop whatever I am doing and play myself one or two games of Box-O. For ignorant readers, perhaps I should explain that this game consists of throwing dice into a small tray and endeavouring to cancel out exactly the digits one to nine by throwing the right numbers. I play myself for enormous stakes, often a million pounds, and on occasions my life. I also take omens. A favourable result will secure me a film or at least a successful medical.

Normally a cautious sort of fellow, there seems no limit to my recklessness when I am with myself. I will sit in a hotel lobby or on a park bench, one leg crossed over the other, and the toe of my shoe pointing at a hall porter or a tree, waiting for the seventeenth to breast the tape. The seventeenth person is the one whom I have promised myself I am to marry, or exchange worldly wealth or age or health, or, if it is a particularly slack afternoon and neither of us is inclined for larger stakes, a head of hair. The seventeenth having passed, I am seldom content with my fate, petitioning myself for three more lives, and promising that if, at the end of this borrowed time I am still not suited, I will cheerfully submit to the death penalty.

What purpose is there in all this, you ask, and why tell us about it? Be patient, gentle reader. How would you have liked to have lived with absurdity all your life? How would you like never to be able to go for a gentle stroll without suddenly being interrupted and dared to reach the pillarbox ahead of the lady with the Pekinese, or the postman on his bicycle, or merely the next bus? I know only too well that if I shrug off the challenge I shall die before I reach the age of seventy-four. Even more difficult are the contests not to arrive

190

ahead of, but to pass at precisely the same moment. I am no judge of pace, and have long ago given up driving a car. Besides, for some reason or other I am not allowed to run. Years ago, when we were both children, and by far the easiest way to avoid the cracks on the pavement was to do so on tiptoe, I was sternly forbidden. Flat-foot or nothing was the rule. It's no wonder, really, that I take so little exercise.

All in all I suppose I am more fortunate than most; as I have already observed I genuinely like myself, and have no reason to believe that the feeling is not reciprocated. There is little of what used to be called jobbing back; both of us realising that we are capable of mischief has kept us out of trouble. Only on very rare occasions do we despair simultaneously. Worse things happen at sea has been our favourite proverb. I like to humour myself. In the final analysis he is the only one on whom I can rely. We were born and we shall die quite alone, save for each other.

Relatively Speaking

I am no longer a nephew. I was bereft of aunts and uncles at the age of sixty-one. I started life with a multitude of these gallant and useful creatures, but death finally removed the last, my uncle Ernest, five years ago. At our ages, neither of us could complain. He was well over eighty, and had had a distinguished career, earning a knighthood, and serving for a time as the Public Trustee. Happening upon him soon after his appointment, I hastened to add my congratulations, and enquire whether he considered planting more rose trees in Hyde Park. 'You have, I am afraid, got hold of the wrong end of the stick as usual,' was his, for once, rather unfriendly riposte. He was right, of course. I have more often than not grasped the wrong end of any stick which has been proffered me. In my youth people were always remarking on it, but now as I grow older and more arrogant I sometimes manage to convince others that mine is the natural hold.

My relatives were never fooled. I was 'Poor Daisy's boy' and 'Poor Daisy' was to be commiserated with. I made matters worse by arguing, extolling Gandhi to my Indian uncle, Communism to my stockbroking uncle, agnosticism to my Roman Catholic aunt. I was determined they should reject me, and they were equally determined never to do so. However outrageous my manners, uncouth my appearance, bizarre my methods of making, or rather not making money, there were still the cards on my birthday, the Postal Orders, and later the modest cheques. They went out of their way to acknowledge and welcome me, should I chance to call on them. When I was selling vacuum cleaners they purchased one at least. When I appeared at a theatre in their neighbourhood they brought a friend to the matinee, and embarrassed me afterwards by extolling my performance. 'You were the butler to the life,' they would inform me. 'Not a large part, but you made it tell.'

Ever ready to indulge me, I refused to indulge them. To me they represented the Mafia, and in this I was influenced by my father, who by virtue of being a compulsive gambler, was excluded from the circle. Capital was sacrosanct, and my father's efforts to breach his marriage settlement and the family's determination to preserve it, developed over the years into a Holy War. My father was wrong of course, and they were right. Nevertheless my sympathy was always on his side. Defeated in his own private battle for sterling, he remained resolutely cheerful, ending his days on potted meat sandwiches, taking care always to lodge within walking distance of a greyhound track and opining that his relatives were all mad.

On the other hand, my aunts and uncles, although palpably sane, never emulated his high spirits. They infected each other with caution, and because there were so many of them, never felt the urge to make friends of their own contemporaries. My mother's immediate reaction to the overtures of would-be acquaintances remained all her life one of deep suspicion.

'Very nice,' she would remark of anyone to whom she had been introduced during the day, 'very nice, but I don't think the sort of person with whom I should have much in common.'

'Why not?' I would ask her. 'I thought them rather jolly.'

'That's the trouble. I don't think I care much for jolly people.' But that wasn't the real reason that she took care to snub them on any subsequent encounter. My mother, like the rest of her family, suffered from the curse of shyness. Shyness is usually inherited. When it runs in families it is the great destroyer of happiness, the insurmountable barrier to fulfilment. It should be demolished before it demolishes.

I have always realised the need to conquer my own shyness, to make friends, to escape from the family, yet the memory of my own uncles and aunts, some of whom have been dead more than twenty years, persists. My aunt Sophie, who read aloud better than anyone I ever heard and who once snatched my father's *Guide to the Turf* from his grasp and flung it into the drawing-room fire. My aunt Betty, who was so enormously stout, and who sat all day listening to the wireless with eyes closed in readiness for any religious service in which she could join. My uncle Edgar who wore stays, and my aunt Connie, who didn't. My uncle Frank, who dressed as a scoutmaster, and my uncle Basil, who seldom bothered to dress at all, and was perpetually moistening his eyelids. There was my uncle who was in love with another man's wife, and my aunt whose husband kept the opera singer in Paris. There was my uncle who was banished to Australia, and I even had an aunt who went into a nunnery, and

193

another who played the cello and danced by herself when the moon was full.

My sister, who got on with them all a great deal better than I did, and who in later years constituted herself into an Aunts' Advice Bureau, stayed the night with me on the eve of Uncle Ernest's funeral, and I learned that she was planning a holiday in Yorkshire, and hoped to visit some remote hamlet where her ancestors (and mine, too) were buried. But whereas she occasionally consults the family tree, and hangs in her house enormous, unrevealing pictures of our great-grandparents, I do all I can to avoid reminding myself that one of them was once Chairman of the London Parcel Company, whatever that could have been.

Cold Comfort

There are people apparently who never have a cold, and I am grateful not to be one of them. Every now and then I need a cold in the head and every now and then, thanks to the bounty of nature, I get one. I am one who welcomes the early warning system going into action. That prickling at the back of the throat, the sudden but unmistakeable urge to halt awhile, to take stock of one's symptoms and to plan ahead. 'I think,' I announce, 'I may be starting a cold.' I find it helpful to make an early announcement, not so much to alert others, but to alert myself. Having decided thus to have a cold, there is a good deal to be decided. Where, for instance, do I intend to have my cold? I dream naturally of bed, to go to bed with a cold, to climb between crisp, clean sheets at about half past eleven in the morning, to arrange the radio on the bedside table, to get others to carry the television up to the bedroom and place it at the foot of the bed. To put out the aspirins and the lemon cordial, to satisfy oneself that there is plenty of whisky in the bottle, and then to close one's eyes and doze fitfully, waking only occasionally to manage a little lunch or tea, or to summon one of the family to enquire bravely what they've been up to and whether it's still raining. To feel a little better and then a little worse, to be not absolutely certain the whole thing isn't going to my chest. Tomorrow, I tell myself, I'll go to bed tomorrow, better still I won't even get up. It's no good walking around and giving everyone else my cold. I find a cold improves my character enormously. I develop what is for me an altogether unnatural concern for others. 'I won't kiss you,' I tell comparative strangers whom indeed I have never kissed before, 'I won't kiss you because I have a little bit of a cold.' They must know as I do how ill I really am, and admire as I do, my own courage and fortitude.

As a child I was put to bed with a cold and although I specialised in bilious attacks, I was always glad of the few extra days' respite from the horrors of childhood. People were nicer to me when I was in bed. I needed people to be nicer to me. I still do, which is why when I am getting a cold, even if I only think I may be getting one, I tell as many people as possible. If I am in a play, the first person I tell is my understudy. I like to see the emotions I have aroused. He rather enjoys playing my part. On the other hand, he quite obviously has no desire to step to stardom over my dead body. 'If I'm not better, I think I shall stay off tomorrow,' I tell him. On the morrow my cold is worse, and I insist on playing.

My cold wakes me in the night. At other times I sleep in a great gulp of unconsciousness, but to put on the light and grope for a handkerchief, and then for my watch, to realise at five in the morning how much of the night still remains for slumber is a luxury usually denied me. It is surprising how well I feel, except for my cold. Deafness no longer worries me. The onslaught of writer's cramp appears to have receded, my digestion is back to square one. In another week my cold will be gone, and I shall have other things to think about, other people to enquire after, but just at the moment I am concentrating all my resources, all my reserves of courage on that most faithful and loyal confidant, myself. I want him to get better, and he usually does.

My life, like most people's lives, has a terrible monotony. That is why nature invented the cold, and why it has been such a success over the years. It provides man with an opportunity to break out, to desert the canteen at lunchtime and visit the chemist's to shop around for some wonder drug without the benefit of skilled medical interference. His cold provides him with a topic of conversation and perhaps a few days' holiday. He will return, having got over his cold – note the phrase – he has surmounted yet another obstacle in the long march to the grave. The common cold is the rainbow in the medical history of a man's life, a sign that he will get better this time. He will get ill again of course, but this time he will recover.

Mr Memory

I knew the hotel should have been somewhere, but turning the car this way and that amid the narrow, winding Cornish lanes, failed to find it and lunched instead in a pub in Tregony. While the landlady cooked the gammon steak, I kept the old gentleman company. He was worried that his pasty was cold. He had bought it earlier in the day at a rival establishment, but now handed it over to be warmed, along with the steak, and then kept forgetting what he had done with it. But what worried him most was my resemblance to Robert Morley. He refused to be comforted. 'You're the spitting image of the fellow,' he persisted. The landlady was anxious to let her dog out for a run, but not until her customer promised he would not try and teach it to sit. 'They excite each other to the point of madness and then the old gentleman gets knocked down.' I left long after closing time and without witnessing the encounter, but what a pleasure it was to be back in Cornwall. There is a soft madness in the air despite the new bungalows.

In Perranporth before the war I used to act in summer stock. The natives encouraged us and came to watch, particularly if we had borrowed anything of theirs with which to dress the stage or the village institute. They loved to see their chairs and tables performing alongside us. Once at rehearsal in my occasional role as director I goaded a colleague beyond endurance, and taking a cricket stump, he smashed up all the furniture already in place for that night's performance. The season never recovered.

I was in Perranporth when war was declared. The *Daily Express* and I were convinced it wasn't going to happen, and when it did, I could think of nothing to do but to bathe, made my way to the beach and hearing a plane overhead, swam for a time underwater. When I surfaced it was to find that Mr. Chamberlain had closed the theatre and one of the cast had been called up. I can see her still, walking towards us across the lawn with a telegram clutched in her hand. 'This is a play,' I told myself, and I was thinking, heaven help me, of *Journey's End* or *The Conquering Hero.* The rest of the company stayed on for a few days and packed up. In the evening we read Government brochures, trying to find ways which might suit our talents. The favourite seemed to be heavy rescue work. I was momentarily attracted to the fire service, but it stressed an ability to climb ladders, and I opted, in theory at any rate, for agricultural work. If none of us rushed to join the Artists' Rifles or the WRAC like some of our colleagues, it was not, I think, that we were cowards, although I do happen to be a coward myself, but that we were in Cornwall. There is a hesitancy in the Cornish air.

But if Perranporth ended in tears, it started triumphantly, and one season Peter Bull, whose project it had been, commissioned a play from me, and I wrote it in thirty-six hours, staying with an aunt at Beachy Head. It was no worse than any of the plays I have written, but I have never ceased to marvel and remind myself of this creative feat. I have always hoped to emulate it, which was the reason perhaps why I had come to Cornwall, and now realise that I should have gone to Beachy Head. 'Eastbourne,' I tell myself, 'is more bracing. This has nothing to do with age.'

But memory has everything to do with age. My own is far from perfect. Naturally I don't expect to have, like Sir Compton Mackenzie, total recall, but I would wish that I had more say in the selection of memorabilia. My memory is quite unable to forget the most trivial incidents which made absolutely no impression on me at the time, and quite unable to recall anything remotely significant. 'How did I feel' I ask memory, 'when my first child was born?' 'I have no idea,' memory replies. 'On that occasion I recorded for you the look not on your face, supposing you to have had a mirror available, nor on your child's face or your wife's face, but on the face of the doctor who delivered him. Similarly, I have recorded the moment in time not when you kissed your wife or baby, but when you shook the congratulatory hand of the obstetrician.'

My mother, in a moment of family crisis, once raised herself from her knees whither she had sunk in despair by clutching hold of the mantelpiece. I do the same thing most evenings when lighting the fire. If you are stout, it's the best way of getting up from such a recumbent position. 'It is not necessary,' I keep telling memory, 'to remind me every evening in that instant of Mother, particularly as you recall her in a moment of deep despair.' If I am to think of my mother every time I light the fire, I would wish for an altogether happier portrait of her, but that is apparently impossible, or what is worse, forbidden.

When the children stopped paddling, we stopped taking them to Cornwall. Instead we chose the Lido, and in the evenings made discreet cultural tours of Venice, eating in the little squares among the American ladies, with the bats swooping from mink to mink. What worried me as a parent on these expeditions was the way the children looked longest and with keenest appreciation not at St. Mark's, but at the cinema posters. They were extremely good at translating the titles, collating them with treats already experienced, or still to come back home at the Odeon. I never expected any of them to become architects, but I couldn't help feeling they were skimping the essentials. It's exactly the same with my memory. 'For heaven's sake take this in properly,' I tell it, as we stand together in front of some august personage, survey Mount Fuji or experience the rare privilege of hearing ourselves speak a few well-chosen words. Alas, on these occasions memory recalls nothing remotely apposite. While I was chatting to Her Majesty it was apparently registering Bernard Delfont's shirtfront. It made an effort with Mount Fuji and failed dismally. Whenever I shut my eyes and demand to be shown this majestic mountain over again, all that it conjures up is a table flap which apparently fascinated memory on the Bullet Train bearing me towards the sacred mountain. Of my after-dinner speeches, it recalls ne'er a syllable. Mind you, there are certain advantages about this latter feat. Not remembering what story I have told before does enable me to repeat it and enjoy it immensely. Perhaps on the whole I have enjoyed everything more in retrospect rather than reality, not having memory there to jog my elbow and contradict. My memory at least knows its place and its place is not by my side, tugging my sleeve, correcting my embellishments. My memory walks two steps behind and I, clutching its sticky, unwilling hand, drag it through the world not as we both remember it, but as one of us imagined and wanted it to be.

My Favourite Deadly Sin

I find it difficult to choose. It is as if I were looking at photographic proofs of a beloved face — my own, naturally. Sloth, Anger, Avarice, Pride, Envy, Lust, Gluttony, all good likenesses, but which is the essential me? Not Anger. I think I had better put a little cross on the back of Anger, or shall I just tear the corner? I am increasingly nervous of my blood pressure these days. A stroke after a good meal is one thing, but after a punch-up on the M4? Besides, there is always the risk I might get the worst of it.

Sloth, Avarice, Vice. I'll hang on to them for a bit. How about Lust? Muggeridge has given it up, why can't I? It's not quite my scene nowadays. I've relied on Lust in the past to enable me to keep a sense of balance, a reminder that I'm not one hundred per cent pure spirit. It's difficult to have an erotic imagination when it's all for real. Corduroy, mackintoshes, gymslips, hotpants. There was a paper once called *London Life,* full of letters describing one-legged ladies wearing pince-nez and carrying dog whips. No one expected that to come true, surely, but I saw her the other day myself outside the Science Museum. No, Lust is definitely out. What does that leave me with? Envy? I can't imagine who compiled this list. How could envy possibly be a sin? Is there some political connotation here, I wonder? The noble exhorting the peasants to get on with the job and leave the wine-tasting to him. If I could only take one vice along with me to a desert island, I don't think I'd fancy Envy. Envy isn't me at all. I believe they have sent along the wrong print. This looks much more like the fellow who always wants to play my parts. I can't think of the name, but I believe they made him a lord, poor chap. I'd better not tear that one up, just put it in the waste paper basket.

Now then, Sloth, Avarice, Pride, Gluttony, it's getting more difficult. They are all good. Pride, well that one presents no problem. I know other people would be proud to be me, but I'm humble.

When the good fairy leant over my crib, she knew her stuff. 'A humble child, this one,' she told her companions, 'give him the lot.'

Sloth, Avarice, Gluttony (getting bored? So am I). It has to be Sloth. Sloth is what keeps a man happy. Women, luckily, are denied it. God gave man the gift of Sloth in exchange for his rib. That's me all right. Sleeping in a topsy-turvy world, the only one really who is the right way up.

A Case History

This dossier was secured by Robert Morley and is the medical case history of a compulsive gambler. No names, no pack drill.

X or * as he prefers to call himself, is a compulsive gambler. A handsome, well-preserved actor in his mid sixties, he still enjoys his share of success on the stage and as an occasional journalist. His introduction to gambling was effected when still a schoolboy when Lord Derby, who was governor of his school, won the Derby with Sansovino. Having wagered a shilling, he was rewarded with nine others and instantly acquired a taste for easy money and, surprisingly, arithmetic. The latter interest, however, waned rapidly, while the former persists to this day. The patient exhibits the typical guilt and temporary withdrawal symptoms following a heavy loss, but does not appear able or indeed willing to rid himself of the compulsion which he admits gives him enormous pleasure and satisfaction.

*'s father and mother separated when * was about sixteen, largely because his father, who was similarly addicted, never seemed able to put down the telephone during racing hours, or once the track was closed provide adequately for the bookmakers, let alone his wife and family. In those days gambling was not officially countenanced in England, save for betting on racehorses, greyhounds and the occasional footballer. *'s father cared little for ball games save for roulette and was forced therefore on frequent occasions to visit Le Touquet or the French Riviera in search of employment. When taxed with the continuing state of insolvency in which the family found itself, he vigorously rejected any suggestion that he had failed to provide adequately for his brood, professing himself a dutiful parent whose sole aim in the various salles privées he frequented was to make a few bob for his loved ones.

On two occasions, * accompanied his father abroad when the latter, having provided himself with all the available spare cash he could lay his hands on, avowed an intention of affording his child an education in a foreign tongue. Both times the expeditions ended abruptly on the Côte d'Azur without one word of French having been exchanged along with the travellers' cheques. Gambling for *'s father was a slippery slope down which he propelled himself on whatever toboggan was immediately available with the utmost cheerfulness and sangfroid for many happy years.

*'s tobogganing is less graceful and a good deal more spasmodic, and there are frequent periods when it is interrupted by the necessity of pursuing his acting career. Until recently, however, he would skip after a Wednesday matinee performance in Shaftesbury Avenue to a casino situated cunningly opposite the stage door, returning periodically to the box office to scoop up any cash lying around. Patrons booking for the attraction in which he was appearing were often startled by the way he would pocket the bread they had just put down in exchange for their tickets and scurry away for another few precious moments at the roulette wheel before it was time to put on the slap once again for the evening performance. * claimed that his performance on these occasions was always improved, for if he won he was in such high spirits that his bonhomie infected players and audience alike whereas, as more often happened, when he had already dissipated the proceeds of his evening chore, he worked twice as hard to ingratiate himself with the public in the vain hope it might return to watch him on the morrow.

Since the late Manningham-Buller drafted a Bill to legalise church bazaars in Britain and found his measure successfully interpreted by casino proprietors as a licence if not to print money at any rate to turn it into plastic counters, life for * and his fellow sufferers in London has become vastly more enjoyable, but also more expensive. It is generally acknowledged by gamblers that it is on the whole wiser not to play on your own doorstep, and if you happen to live in Nice it will be cheaper for you to fly to London for a splurge and vice versa. Thus * has from time to time barred himself from scenes of past disaster on his native soil by writing courteous notes to unknown (at any rate to him) committees of various London establishments, offering his resignation and requesting that the doorman should politely refuse him admission should he present himself in future. There are a good many gambling clubs in London and few of them by now haven't at least one if not two of these epistles frugally stowed away, not for reference, but for eventual sale at Sotheby's.

There are not many letters of *'s on other subjects extant.

Last year * took even sterner measures and circulated all the clubs of which he might or might not have been a member at the time, explaining that under the terms of a peace treaty agreed with his accountants, no cheque of his was valid unless it bore two signatures. This ingenious falsehood has for the last year kept him out of trouble on his home ground, and peace once again reigns at the box office of any theatre in which he is performing.

It is worth noting perhaps that the patient's addiction is almost entirely concerned with roulette, a game of absolutely no skill whatsoever and at which no successful system of winning has ever been devised; thus he is not required either to pit his wits or employ his minimal mathematical knowledge, he is always searching for the end of the rainbow and the crock of gold.

Not that he expects ever to grasp it, or wishes to do so, for then he might be tempted to stop. In Vegas recently *'s attention was caught by an old lady who sat opposite him at the table and played, like himself, for long hours at a stretch. She would sometimes wander off to get more money at the caisse or very occasionally to cash in some chips, and during her absence her chair was uptilted and the white chips reserved for her return. This is unusual at Vegas, even for so steady a customer, and *'s concentration was momentarily diverted from the game to enquire her name of the croupier, and why she was afforded favourite nation status. 'She owns the joint,' he was told. 'Her old man died and left her the premises.' A widow who inherits a casino and continues to play against herself for six hours at a stretch. 'I realised,' * told me, 'that there was no risk of my giving up the game entirely. I was looking across the table into a mirror.'

ROBERT MORLEY WRITES

The moral of this fascinating case history is obvious. If you must gamble, travel. The corollary is also true: if you must travel, gamble. There is no better way of reorientating yourself after a long flight than an evening, or better still a day or two in a casino, where time does not exist. As for the patient, his doctor recommended periodic visits to foreign casinos. Total withdrawal in his case might be injurious and he might even pine away. An effort will have to be made before too late to obtain a membership for him in a Darby and Joan Bingo Club.

Past Twelve O'Clock and All's Well

It's not just the face, it's the shape. People look twice at a fat man. Goodness, they tell themselves, I wouldn't care to sit next to him on a bus. Goodness, it's Robert Morley. Goodness. I am fortunate in being self-conscious in the worst possible way. I welcome the encounters. There are happy games to be played on the street corner, in the railway carriage, in the elevator. It would be easy to tell the man who is sure I must have lived once in Cheadle or Chicago why my face is familiar, but I seldom do. I pretend to share his perplexity. 'How strange,' I tell him, 'for I too feel we must have met before. Could it be Colchester? Have you ever lived in Colchester?'

There is the man whose wife has prompted him to come over to my table in the restaurant, and ask my name. 'She thinks you're an actor.' I seldom deny it. On the other hand, I am not always forthcoming, seeking to prolong his embarrassment, postponing the inevitable anti-climax. I know that sooner or later I will have to supply the information his wife demands, and that when I do so, one name will not suffice. If I say 'Morley', he's almost certain to riposte 'Christopher Morley', and when I tell him 'Robert Morley', he will agree. 'That's right,' he will tell me happily, shake my hand and retire. One day, of course, I shall forget my name and pine for reassurance, wondering why in the past I always flinched when 'That's right' was said.

There are certain things I do, and other things I don't do. I never accept a cloakroom ticket. I never jump a queue, but I never stand in one in a restaurant. If the maître d'hotel doesn't remember I've booked a table when I haven't, and suggests I wait, I am off like a flash. 'Some other evening when you're not so busy,' I tell him. There are more ways than one of putting in the boot. I over-tip taxi-drivers. An actor who doesn't keep on good terms with taxi-drivers doesn't know his business. Taxis usually stop when I hail them, always when I am crossing the road. On days when old films of mine have been shown the night before on the box, I wear a hat. I don't say it disguises me, I am careful nothing shall do that, but it stops a certain number of the casual hails from passing lorry-drivers. I enjoy being hailed by lorry-drivers, but I am aware of my responsibility as a citizen to encourage careful driving.

I will sign anything unless I am in a hurry or in a crowd. In point of fact I will sign anything when I'm in a hurry as long as the man or woman or child — I hesitate to use the word fan — keeps up with me. The reason most people ask for an autograph on the back of their cheque book or the margin of a newspaper is not because they collect autographs or admire me as an actor, but because someone somewhere will be vaguely interested when they show them my name on a cigarette packet. They won't be able to read it, but no matter.

When the elderly demand an autograph, it is never for themselves, always for their little niece. In their request is the implication that we are both engaged on good works. 'Little Alice,' they tell me, 'will be so thrilled.' I am thankful I am not there to witness little Alice's disappointment, as she reaches out her hand for the surprise, anticipating a candy bar, and receives a race-card programme with a name which she couldn't read even if she'd heard of it, scrawled in the margin.

On programmes I always write my name meticulously and add good wishes. Paying customers are entitled to privilege. I am ready to pose for them when they linger outside the stage door with a camera, agreeing to the suggestion that their loved ones should stand beside me. 'This is Moira in front of the Trevi Fontana, and here she is again beside Robert Morley.'

Long, long ago when I first went into 'the Business', the carriage in which I travelled to Weymouth bore a reserved label on which was written 'And So To Bed Blue Company'. Every time the train stopped I stared out at would-be fellow travellers, daring them to try the handle. It cost sixteen shillings to go from London to Weymouth in those days, and I was so proud that someone should have thought me worth carting around, particularly as I only had one line to deliver. 'Past twelve o'clock, and all's well.' After the matinée I used to have tea at Fullers, because people who went to matinées went to Fullers afterwards and I wanted to be recognised as the night watchman. I could never bear to be recognised before a performance. I had disembarked on too many platforms with a group of fellow optimists, and attempted to take too many Pier Heads by storm.

206

Why, I would ask myself, would anyone ever pay to see this lot? And very often of course, they didn't. Managers in those days were very strict on actors not fraternising. Woe betide any performer they caught out front. To be seen in the stalls bar meant instant dismissal. I still cross the road and slink past any theatre in which I am appearing.

I asked my son the other day how tiresome it had been to have had such a noisy father, perpetually demanding the attention of the head waiter. 'Well, we got the service,' he told me. On the whole I have done what I wanted to do, what most men want to do, made my mark. It has no particular significance. Like me, its shape leaves a great deal to be desired. It was fun while it lasted. It won't last very long. I am content.

ACKNOWLEDGEMENTS

Thanks are due to the editors of the following publications in which some of these pieces originally appeared: *Punch* (pp. 1, 4, 14, 19, 171, 181, 183, 186, 200, 202); *Tatler* (pp. 22, 42, 49, 52, 56, 71, 77, 82, 85, 114, 126, 129, 140, 152, 174, 189, 192, 195, 197); *Evening News* (pp. 93, 99); *The Observer* Magazine (pp. 26, 111, 116, 145, 168, 205); *World Medicine* (p. 149); *Playboy* Magazine (pp. 91, 104 — 'Marco Roly-Poly Meets the Mysterious East', copyright (c) 1969 by *Playboy;* p. 155 — 'The Grand Hotels', copyright (c) 1969 by *Playboy;* p. 61 — 'Take Me To Your Tailor', copyright (c) 1971 by *Playboy;* p. 132 — 'Mr Morley Meets the Frog', copyright (c) 1971 by *Playboy*).